All the people in the land of Pipella were scared of Silgar. When he roared, everyone hid. He set their houses on fire. He took away their children and ate them.

Princess Tala was the real King's daughter. She was scared of Silgar. When he roared, she hid under Kalim's wings. Kalim was her dragon friend. He was a red dragon, and Tala felt safe under his soft, red wings.

"I hate Silgar," Tala said. "He took my father away to his cave. All the people of Pipella are scared of Silgar. I'd do anything to make him go away."

"Anything?" Kalim looked at her with his soft, brown eyes. "Even if it made you scared?"

"Do you know who can stop him, Kalim?"

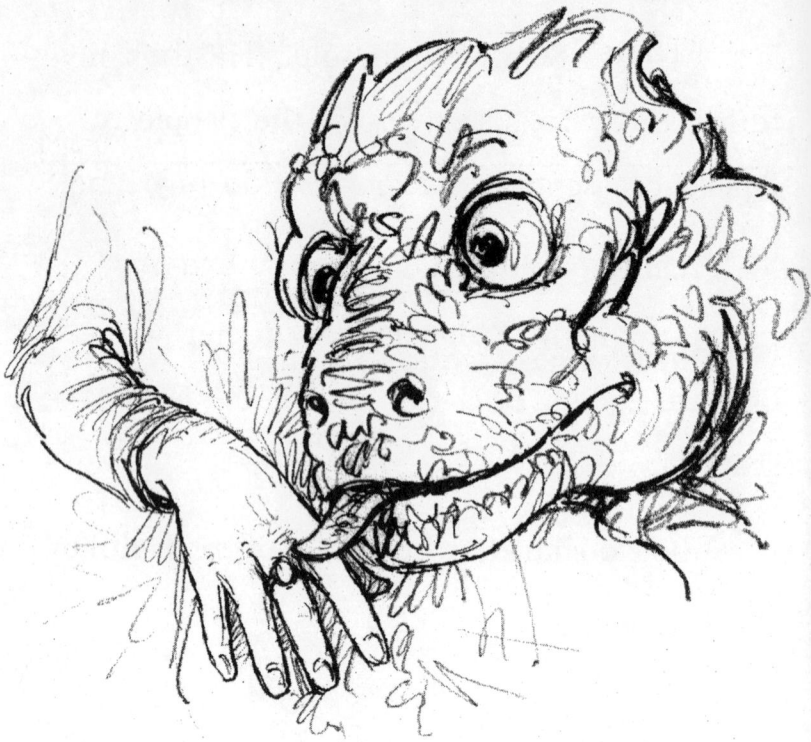

"You can do it, Tala," said Kalim, "but you'll have to be brave."

"Me? What can I do?" she asked.

Kalim put his nose on her hand, and licked her silver ring. It was the ring her father gave her just before Silgar took him away.

"There's a dragon song," Kalim said.

"I'll sing a song of a Princess brave,

Who fights a Dragon in his cave.

With the help of a silver ring,

The Princess brave will save the King."

"Is that about me?" Tala asked.

Kalim nodded his head. Tala was
scared. The song said she would have to
fight a dragon. She had never had to fight
anything before.

"You must go to Silgar's cave," Kalim
told her. "It's on the other side of the
Wild Wood."

"But Wood Demons live in the Wild Wood," Tala said.

"I'll go with you," said Kalim, "and you have the ring."

"But what will I do with the ring?" asked Tala. "How will it help?"

"When the time comes you will know," said Kalim.

It was getting dark when they got to the Wild Wood. Tala could hear strange sounds. She held on to Kalim's wing. He was scared, too.

They walked faster. Soon they were deep in the Wild Wood. Tala heard footsteps. She looked behind them, but she couldn't see any Wood Demons. It was so dark that she couldn't see anything.

"I'm scared, Kalim," said Tala. "It's too dark. We can't see. We'll get lost and the Wood Demons will get us."

"Do you want to give up?" asked Kalim.

Tala stopped walking. "No," she said at last. "We must go on."

"Look at your ring," said Kalim.

Tala looked at the silver ring. It was glowing. When she held up the ring, she could see the way.

"Look, Kalim," she said. "The light from the ring will help us."

There was a roar behind them.

"Run, Kalim!" she cried. They ran as fast as they could. Tala saw the end of the Wild Wood, but the footsteps were getting closer. Just as they got to the end of the wood, she heard another loud, angry roar.

"They'll get us!" shouted Tala.

"No, they won't!" Kalim told her.
"The Wood Demons can't leave the Wild
Wood. We're safe – for now!"

Then Kalim saw a deep cave in the hill.

"Look!" he said. "There's Silgar's cave."

They climbed up the hill. There was
smoke coming from the cave. They heard a
loud roar.

"He's coming!" said Tala. "I'm scared,
Kalim."

"Do you want to give up?" asked Kalim.

Tala stopped climbing. "No," she said at
last. "We must go on!"

Tala held up her ring. She was so
scared her hand was shaking, but the ring
had started to glow.

"Silgar!" shouted Tala. "I have come to fight you!"

Tala saw flames and smoke. Suddenly, Silgar was standing in front of her.

"Who dares to fight Silgar?" he roared. He was enormous. Flames came out of his mouth, and he had long, sharp claws.

"I am Tala of Pipella!" cried the Princess.

He roared again. Tala and Kalim backed away.

"Use the ring, Tala," said Kalim.

Tala felt the ring getting hot. It was glowing, too. She held up her hand. "By the power of this silver ring, I destroy you, Silgar."

The silver ring got hotter and hotter. It glowed brighter and brighter. Suddenly, a beam of light shot out of the ring.

Silgar roared in pain. The light hit him again, and he fell down. He was dead.

"He's dead!" shouted Tala.

"Now Pipella will be safe again!" said Kalim. "Thanks to you, Tala."

"It was the ring!" Tala said.

"No, Tala," said a voice. "You did it because you didn't give up."

"Father!" shouted Tala. "You're safe!"

She ran up to the King, and he hugged her.

Other Worlds

Alan Alone

by **David Clayton**

illustrated by **Derek Brazell**

The Silver Ring

by **Linda Strachan**

illustrated by **Kenny McKendry**

Alan Alone

by David Clayton

Alan looked across the space station where he lived. In the middle was an enormous park. The park was called the Ark. Alan's dad looked after the Ark. Robots helped him.

The Ark was like a big zoo. Lots of animals had been saved from Earth. They lived in the Ark. It was not safe for the animals or people to live on Earth anymore.

Alan was lonely. There was nothing to do. He could not go down into the Ark. Dad had told Alan never to go there. Alan didn't know why. No other people lived on the space station. They lived on other space stations nearby. Alan didn't have any friends. He was alone.

Alan went back to his room. He was not happy. He had a warm room and a soft bed. He had good food and nice clothes. He had everything he wanted. But he was not happy at all.

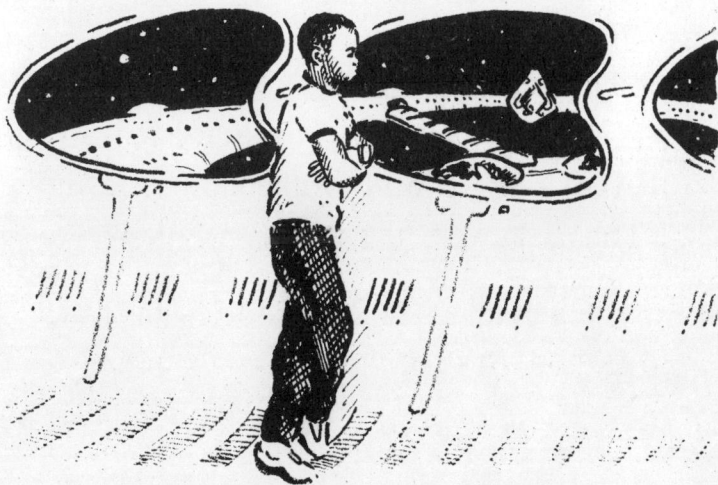

Suddenly, he heard his dad's voice.

"Time to eat your lunch, Alan," said Dad. "What do you want?"

A list of food came up on the big screen. Alan didn't look at it.

"I want you here, Dad," said Alan.

Alan's dad was not really in the room. His dad was just on video. Alan hadn't seen his real dad for two days. He didn't know where his dad was. Something must be wrong, but Alan didn't know what.

"Time to play Space Crash," said the screen.

Alan got up and walked out. He did not eat lunch. He did not play Space Crash. He had to find his dad – he just had to.

Then Alan got a big surprise. He heard some dogs barking. A small door to the Ark was open. Dad had told Alan never to go into the Ark. But Alan had to find Dad.

Alan went into the Ark. But he had made a big mistake. The dogs in the Ark were not pets. They would kill him if they saw him. There were lots of them. They hadn't seen Alan yet. If they did, he would be in big trouble.

"Now I know why you told me not to come here, Dad," said Alan softly.

Then he saw a way past the dogs. There was a rope ladder. It went high up into the trees. Alan tip-toed to the ladder. Suddenly, his dad's voice came on the radio.

"Alan ... Alan ... come in ... Al ... Alan."

"Dad!" shouted Alan.

The dogs heard Alan shout. They
started running. Alan jumped on to the
rope ladder. The radio fell out of his hand.

"No!" shouted Alan.

Alan was scared. He had lost his
radio. Now Alan couldn't tell Dad where
he was. Dad would never find him.

Alan climbed up the tree. It was very high. He didn't look down. He went along a branch. The branch was long. Alan went a long way. He didn't look down. Suddenly, Alan saw a snake ... and the snake saw Alan. He was scared. He had to let go of the branch. He had to get away from the snake. Alan looked down. There was deep water below him. Alan jumped into it.

The water swept Alan away. He was heading for a dark tunnel.

"HELP!" shouted Alan.

The water was running faster and faster. It swept Alan into the tunnel. The air was growing hotter and hotter. He heard a sound like thunder. It was getting louder and louder. Alan was heading for a waterfall. Below the waterfall was a big pool. In the pool there were crocodiles. It was the end of Alan's journey. It was the end of his life.

"I'm going to die!" shouted Alan.

Then, suddenly, the tunnel was full of
light. Suddenly, alarms were sounding.
Suddenly, a gate was rising and the water
level was falling.

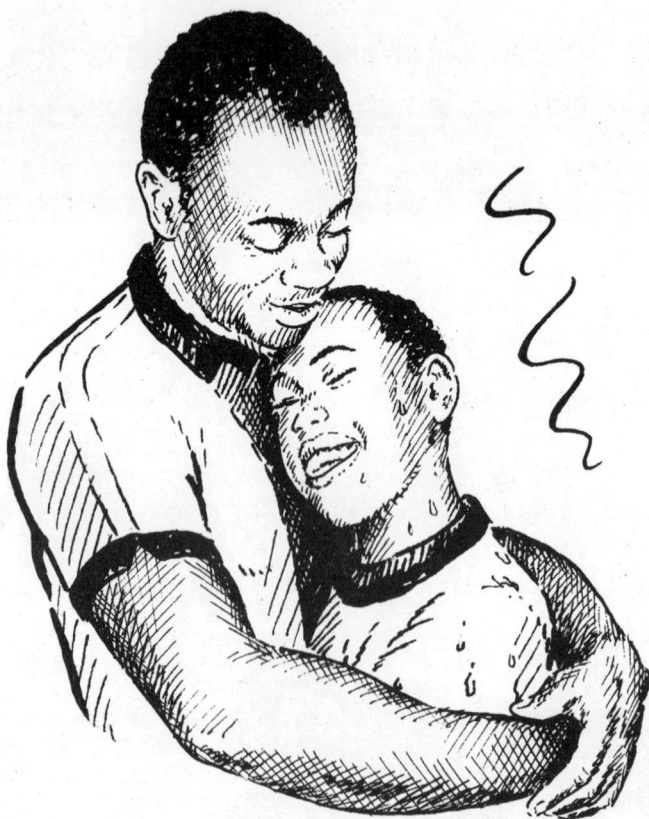

"What's happening?" shouted Alan.

A door opened in the wall. Strong hands grabbed Alan. It was Dad. Dad had found him. Alan hugged his dad hard.

"I'm sorry Dad!" cried Alan. "I know you told me not to go into the Ark, but I just had to find you. I was so alone up there."

"I'm sorry, Alan," said Dad. "I didn't know I would be gone so long. I was down the other end of the space station when Earth Command called me. They asked me to do an important job. I tried to call you, but the radio was down."

"What was the important job, Dad?" said Alan.

"I had to check out the whole station one last time. The Earth is safe again, Alan. Everyone is going back. We can take the animals back, at last."

Alan laughed.

"That's great news!" he said.

Alan and his dad had lived on the Ark for six years and seventeen days. Now, they were going home.

The Silver Ring

by Linda Strachan

Long ago and far away, there was a land
called Pipella. It was a land of dragons
and magic. It was a time of great danger.

One big, black dragon wanted to be king. The dragon took the real King, and kept him in his cave. The dragon was called Silgar.

Petit Pont 2

Teacher's Guide

Published by Eclipse Books

First published in 2006

Eclipse Books, St John's Court, 8 Tyers Gate, London SE1 3HX

ISBN 0-9548108-6-4

Illustrations by HL Studios, 17 Fenlock Court, Blenheim Office Park, Long Hanborough, Oxford, OX29 8LN

Design and layout by HL Studios, 17 Fenlock Court, Blenheim Office Park, Long Hanborough, Oxford, OX29 8LN

Printed by Planit Print and Design

Contents

Introduction

Welcome to Petit Pont 2!

Teachers familiar with *Petit Pont* scarcely need an introduction. The broad principles underlying *Petit Pont 1* are pursued here. They can be summarized as follows:

- to provide an **enjoyable language learning experience**;
- to lay down reliable **foundations for future learning**;
- to help children develop a **tolerance** and an **appreciation** of what is **different** in another **culture**;
- to help them develop both **collaborative skills** and **autonomy** as learners.

When teaching another language, fun is not just something that can be injected to make the process more palatable. At the very heart of language learning are the pleasures of role-playing, play acting, pretending. But there is also a great sense of achievement simply in being able to say "Happy birthday!", "Bless you!" or "Sorry" in another language. Remember the pleasure (or was it surprise?) you first felt when understanding a foreigner's directions actually got you to the right place. Think of the extraordinary satisfaction when what at first sounded like just a stream of sounds began to break down into recognizable words and to *make sense*. If making contact is what being human is all about, and if language is arguably our crowning achievement, then **overcoming language barriers must be one of our greatest potential triumphs**.

But learning a language has more to offer than just the language you are learning. It has been established beyond question that the benefits of learning another language go well beyond the practical convenience of being able to buy the right bus ticket in Calais. It helps to develop a kind of **mental agility**. It does for the mind what physical exercise does for the body. This is no doubt partly to do with its code cracking qualities, partly with **memory training**. But it is also related to **problem solving** and **quick thinking** in general.

Many of the strategies needed when trying to operate in a foreign language, on the other hand, are only variations of those we employ instinctively when using our own:

- Using **facial expressions** and **gestures**;
- Finding **alternative ways** of saying something;
- **Playing for time** – I mean, you know, kind of like… hesitating;
- **Questioning**, asking for clarification, feeling for clues;
- And probably most important of all: **guessing**.

These are **essential language skills**, not just panic measures, and need to be acknowledged, practised and praised.

With *Petit Pont 2* children will:

- increase their ability to **express themselves** and to **understand** both **spoken** and **written** French.
- take steps towards being able to **write** whole sentences.

4

- cover the language and topics of the **Key Stage 2 Scheme of Work** and reflect the spirit and philosophy of the **5 – 14 guidelines**.
- be following a methodology that fully supports the principles, values and strands of the **Key Stage 2 Framework**.

The four skills

Much has been written and said about the relationship between the skills of listening, speaking, reading and writing. Most people's main motivation for learning a foreign language is to be able to communicate orally. Reading comes some way behind that, and writing comes a very distant third. This approach is 'natural', and as teachers we would do well to take account of how it reflects the order in which children have learned their 'native' or first language. However, learners beyond the infant stage also find it helpful, if not indispensable, to **see** the written word as a method of memorizing new knowledge, though they may quite properly not be concerned about being able to spell it accurately. Most primary school children take pleasure in being able to understand the written language, and this will apply to short pieces of written French. It is also a fundamental literacy skill to learn to build up an understanding of the relationship between French sounds and spelling, which will help them to become more independent learners, for example in predicting how to pronounce new words.

The use of ICT strengthens the case for the inclusion of reading and writing at an early stage. Without any doubt, the best way of motivating children to write is to set up a correspondence by **email with French speakers** of their own age. Before long, they will be sending each other documents and recommending websites that will stretch their reading to new heights!

Certainly, one of the teacher's key challenges is to strike the right **balance between encouraging communication and fostering accuracy**. It may not matter to a French person whether what you say is grammatically correct, as long as they can understand you, but most people do derive some satisfaction from knowing they are using a language correctly. What makes the teacher's job harder is that this balance between communication and accuracy varies from individual to individual. But by building on each child's successes and always **reinforcing the positive**, you should work towards a situation where children themselves become more and more **motivated** to get things right.

Pronunciation

It is a curious fact that most of us, while developing our knowledge of a foreign language, somehow fail to improve our accent or our pronunciation. Though children are more **open to imitation** and have a **'better ear'**, they too will stop trying to improve their pronunciation unless consciously encouraged to do so. Don't assume that making the right noises is only something that needs to be practised at the beginning. **In every unit of Petit Pont there is a feature focussing on a particular sound** (look for the blue parrot). But also make a habit of drawing their attention to pronunciation in general, praising good examples and, when errors occur, encouraging them or others to come up with the correct pronunciation rather than supplying it yourself.

Don't worry if your own accent is less than perfect. The audio CD and the CD-ROM will serve as a model for your pupils.

Grammar

Grammar has had a bad press but it has its place in foreign language learning. It's true that we all learned our own language without reference to grammar. But children learning a second language in school do not have the advantage of hearing and using it all day every day. For this reason, gaining a conscious understanding of how it works can save time and help them make progress. Try to allow questions about grammar to *emerge* from the language being used. Encourage children to work out for themselves what is happening and to think in terms of discovering 'patterns' rather than 'rules'. The grammar points occurring in Petit Pont 2, together with ideas for explaining them and ways of practising them, are dealt with as they arise throughout this Guide.

Recycling language

Throughout Petit Pont, language once introduced is **systematically recycled** to prevent children forgetting what they have learned. In the same way, the CD-ROM does not just focus on the new language of each unit, but **re-introduces** words from previous units to keep them fresh in children's minds.

The materials

Different teachers teach in different ways. Every class is different from the next. And different schools devote different amounts of time to languages. For all these reasons, **Petit Pont is designed to be a very flexible resource**. It offers a range of materials, all interrelated, from which you can select those elements which you think will best serve your purposes. **It caters to a variety of learning styles, including the kinaesthetic.** Using all the stage 2 components will provide you with plenty of material for two years. But however selective you need to be, it is recommended that you take the time to read through the notes before embarking on a unit. This will give you an overview of all the ideas and resources at your disposal, including activities that require no resources at all beyond you and your pupils!

The pupil's book

Like the first book, this is a **highly visual resource**, designed to bring alive the characters and places of Petit Pont. As well as enjoying its range of activities, puzzles, songs, poems and games, children benefit from having a book which lays out clearly what they are learning and which they can look back over. The **wordlist** at the end is comprehensive and provides **translations of all the words that occur in the text**.

The audio CD

This contains **all the dialogues, poems, songs and stories featured in the pupil's book**. The speech is carefully paced and recorded by authentic French speakers. Activities accompanied by a recording are indicated in the book by a **CD symbol** 🔘 showing a track number.

The poems and songs

Of the things we tend to remember from our own early language learning, rhymes and songs are by far the most enduring – even if we are not always sure what they are about! Try to treat them not as light relief but as **integral teaching tools**. They should be used to focus on **pronunciation, rhythm and intonation**. Learning them by heart can give children a great sense of achievement – and stay with them for life!

A **karaoke version of each of the songs**, with a bouncing ball moving along the words as a guide, is available on the Interactive Whiteboard version of the CD-ROM.

Storytelling

Now that children's recognition vocabulary has increased and their ear has 'tuned in' more to the language, they should be more able than ever to enjoy listening to a story. As in Petit Pont 1, **the stories here are carefully built around the words and structures they have been learning and using, thus making any special preparation unnecessary**. The emphasis is still on understanding the spoken language rather than reading a text. You can either read the stories yourself, using the text in this Teacher's Guide, or play the recording of them on the audio CD. The ideal is probably a combination of the two, allowing children to listen to the recording as a follow-up to hearing it told in class. The **pictures** in the book (also available on the interactive whiteboard version of the CD-ROM) not only make the whole thing more fun but also provide important **visual clues** to aid understanding.

6

The stories can be exploited in a number of ways:
- allocate children **roles** in the story which they then **act out** as it is retold;
- rehearse or improvise a **puppet show** based on the story;
- read out the story with certain **key words changed** which children have to spot, and correct, as it goes along;
- select or show **one illustration at a time** (**out of sequence**) and ask children to produce a suitable **sentence** or **piece of dialogue** to go with it;
- children can **illustrate** a scene from the story and **write a suitable caption** or text;
- if you want children to handle the written text, cut it up into **sections** for them to **put together** in the **correct sequence**.

Health warning: too much exploitation can kill a good story!

The CD-ROM

This exists in three versions and is designed for use:
- on the interactive whiteboard (Whiteboard Site Licence – contains extra class activities);
- on individual computers at school (Network Site Licence);
- by children at home (Single User Licence).

These three functions are not mutually exclusive.

A common pattern followed by teachers is to present and practise language in class using certain of the activities, then to allow children time on their own either to consolidate these or to move on to subsequent activities.

N.B. Because they can be used in different ways and at different times, **the CD-ROM activities are not always referred to in the proposed teaching sequence itself**. Instead, a short description of them is given at the start of every unit – but of course this is no substitute for trying them out for yourself!

Among the many things this resource offers are:
- the familiar, **French setting**, always keeping **language in context**;
- **immediate feedback**: children know straight away whether they've got something right;
- the **option** always to **try again**;
- the ability to **learn through mistakes** – through trial and error;
- the **simultaneous** presentation (as in real life) of **image** and **sound**, plus, where appropriate, the **written word**;
- a graphic quality that addresses the potential mismatch between children's **visual sophistication** and the **relatively simple level of the language** they are handling;
- **independence**: a help button is at hand in case children are not sure what to do, as is the option to see and hear a **translation of any of the instructions**. In addition, the audio **wordlist** includes every word occurring in the CD-ROM;
- a means of **recycling and reinforcing** language in such a **varied way** that children do not get bored with its limited content;
- the introduction, in some activities, of the **element of timing** to make things more **challenging** and add extra fun;
- a potential **link between home and school**. Children will be keen to continue 'playing' on Petit Pont in their own time. Hints and suggestions as to how parents can support their children's learning are available free on the website **www.eclipsebooks.com/petitpont**

The *activités orales* on the CD-ROM provide the opportunity for pupils to **record their own voices into dialogues using the key language** of each unit. They can compare their pronunciation with the original and re-record it at any time – or if they prefer they can invent their own lines.

The **virtual reality adventure game** *Voyage dans un autre monde* is designed as a **reward** for success in the unit activities and is therefore (except on the whiteboard CD-

ROM) only accessible after scoring 50% of the available points. Level 1 is accessible after doing units 1 and 2; level 2 after doing units 3 and 4; level 3 after doing units 5 and 6; and level 4 after doing units 7 and 8. This 50% bar can be modified by following the instructions on the CD-ROM inlay. **Understanding certain key elements of language is essential for making progress in the game, whilst other bits of dialogue are subtitled in English.**

Use of the target language

The more you can conduct your whole lesson in French, the more children will take it seriously as **a genuine means of communication**.

The instructions for activities in the book, the CD-ROM and the copymasters are all in French. Further expressions useful in the classroom are given in the list below. If you are the class teacher, there are many opportunities for introducing French into other subject areas – from calling the register and writing the date, to praising and encouraging or giving instructions in P.E.

However, if children have questions or contributions they want to make during the lesson, it is unreasonable to refuse them simply because they are not in French.

Classroom language

Teacher to children

S'il te plaît/ S'il vous plaît.	Please (singular & plural)
Assieds-toi/ Asseyez-vous.	Sit down. (singular & plural)
Lève-toi/ Levez-vous.	Stand up. (singular & plural)
Levez la main.	Put your hands up.
Formez un cercle.	Make a circle.
Fais attention/ Faites attention.	Pay attention. (singular & plural)
Ecoutez (bien).	Listen (carefully).
Regardez le tableau/ le livre.	Look at the board/ the book.
Répète/ Répétez.	Say it again. (singular & plural)
Tous ensemble.	All together.
Devinez.	Have a guess.
Ouvrez vos livres (à la page 12).	Open your books (at page 12).
Prenez vos stylos.	Get out your pen.
Dis-le/ dites-le en français.	Say it in French (singular & plural).
Comment dit-on «who» en français?	How do you say «who» in French?
Travaillez avec votre partenaire.	Work with your partner.
Sortez vos affaires/ vos livres.	Get out your things/ your books.
Du calme.	Settle down.
Qui sait?	Who knows?
Allez.	Come on.
Calmez-vous.	Settle down.
Arrête/ Arrêtez!	Stop it! (singular & plural)
Ça suffit!	That's enough!
Taisez-vous!	Be quiet!
Silence!	Silence!

Children to teacher

Maître/ Maîtresse.	Sir/ Miss.
S'il vous plaît.	Please.
Je ne comprends pas.	I don't understand.
Je ne sais pas.	I don't know.
S'il vous plaît, vous pouvez répéter?	Can you repeat that, please?
Que veut dire « ... »?	What does « ... » mean?
Désolé(e).	Sorry.
Je n'ai pas de livre/ de crayon.	I haven't got a book/ a pencil.

Team games

You may like to create regular teams within the class to compete with each other when playing flashcard or other games. Teams could be given names such as *les bleus, les blancs* and *les rouges.*

Using the flashcards

Flashcards, available on the separate Copymasters and Flashcards CD-ROM, can be used for **introducing, practising or linking** separate items of language.

Below are some of the most effective ways they can be used. This list can be referred to whenever flashcard games are recommended in the course of the units.

- Show, name and ask class/ individuals to repeat.
- Show a card and ask, for example: *C'est un jean? Oui ou non?*
- Show a card. Children have to give the French.
- Pit pairs of children or teams against each other. Show a card quickly. The first person or team to answer gets a point.
- Display or stick up on the board a number of pictures. When you name one, a volunteer or designated representative of competing teams has to point to the correct picture as fast as possible.
- Show picture and say either the right or the wrong name. Children repeat only if it is the right one.
- Give one or two flashcards to each of a row of children standing in front of the class. When you or a volunteer name a card the appropriate child has to hold it up.
- Line up or stick on the board at least five cards. Call up a volunteer who covers his/ her eyes while you or another child remove one. The volunteer has to name the thing that is missing (a version of Kim's Game).
- Show part of picture and ask class/ individual to guess what it is.
- Show a series of flashcards one at a time, standing or sticking up each one with its back to the class, so they have to remember which one is where. Children then have to locate them as you name them.
- Allocate different cards to a group of children in front of the class. Name two of the pictures. The children with those pictures have to exchange them as fast as they can.
- Show two flashcards from different topic areas and challenge children (in teams) to produce a sentence or dialogue that links them together. Flashcards from Petit Pont 1 can profitably be re-used for this.
- Distribute a number of flashcards. Say: *"Quelque chose qui commence par...."* and name a letter of the alphabet. Anyone who has a picture of something beginning with that letter holds it up or calls out its name.

List of flashcards

Unit nº.	Flashcard nºs.	
Unit 1	1	le cinéma
	2	le centre commercial
	3	la rivière
	4	la boulangerie
	5	tourne à gauche
	6	tourne à droite
	7	va tout droit
	8	traverse le pont
Unit 2	9	il fait beau
	10	il fait gris
	11	il fait chaud
	12	il fait froid
	13	il pleut
	14	il neige
	15	nord, sud, est, ouest

Unit 4	16	le foot
	17	le basket
	18	le tennis
	19	le rugby
	20	le vélo
	21	la natation
	22	la danse
	23	la gymnastique
Unit 5	24	un coca
	25	un jus d'orange
	26	une limonade
	27	un café
	28	un thé
	29	un sandwich au jambon
	30	un sandwich au fromage
	31	un paquet de chips
	32	une glace (menthe)
	33	une glace (fraise)
	34	une glace (vanille)
	35	une glace (chocolat)
	36	une glace (citron)
Unit 6	37	un pull
	38	un jean
	39	une jupe
	40	un sweat
	41	une robe
	42	un pantalon
	43	une chemise
	44	un t-shirt
	45	des chaussures
	46	des baskets
	47	une casquette
Unit 7	48	je me lève
	49	je vais à l'école
	50	je mange à la cantine
	51	je rentre à la maison
	52	je vais au lit
	53	le français
	54	la géographie
	55	l'anglais
	56	les sciences
	57	l'histoire
	58	le sport
	59	la musique
	60	l'art plastique
	61	les maths
	62	une baguette
	63	un croissant
	64	un pain aux raisins
	65	un pain au chocolat
	66	la boulangerie
	67	la boucherie
	68	l'épicerie
	69	la pharmacie
	70	le supermarché

One more game

'Follow-me' cards are useful and popular **for starter and plenary activities**, and provide a good way of **keeping alive key language** from previous topics.

You need to devise a series of questions and answers – as many questions as there are pupils in the class. You then create a series of cards, of which the first contains just the first question on your list, the second contains the answer to that and the next question, and so on. Thus a typical card will look like this:

> *Il fait froid.*
>
> *Où vas-tu?*

Distribute the cards randomly around the class. The child with the first, 'question-only' card begins by reading out their question, e.g. *Quel temps fait-il?* Everyone else looks at their card and the child with the appropriate answer calls it out and then reads aloud **his/ her** question, and so on. As an activity, besides being fun, this has the advantage that everyone has to pay attention to each other. It can offer a good opportunity to work on pronunciation, and children can have even more fun if you time the activity.

The same game can be played using simple sums, e.g.

> 24
> 10 + 5

> 15
> 13 + 7

> 20
> 5 + 6

or questions involving similar sequencing with words, such as:

> *juillet*
> *le mois après mars.*

> *avril*
> *le jour après lundi.*

> *mardi*
> *le nombre après onze.*

The copymasters

These are **not just 'extras'**. They include such things as **pairwork games** (pelmanism, and word and picture dominoes) which are not replicated elsewhere in the materials. They are flagged throughout this guide at the point where their use is most appropriate, together with a miniature showing what they look like.

All the **copymasters are editable**, allowing you to **customize** them if you wish. For example, the font size can be increased, or a menu of answers can be modified or removed in order to create different levels of challenge for different members of the class.

The last eight copymasters (n°s. 18 – 25) are **personal record sheets** for self-evaluation, and are designed to be completed by pupils at the end of each unit. The targets on these can similarly be amended to suit the ability of a particular class or individuals.

List of copymasters

Unit n°.	Copymaster n°s.	Title
1	1	*La nouvelle fille*
	2	*Plan de Petit Pont*
2	3	*Mon journal du temps*
	4	*Carte postale*
3	5	*Loto horaire*
	6	*Aujourd'hui*
4	7	*Sondage sur les sports*
	8	*Jeu de paires*
5	9	*Combien d'euros?*
	10	*Ma salière*
	11	*Email*
6	12	Les dominoes
	13	*Qui porte quoi?*
7	14	*Kit phrases*
	15	*Le tour de Petit pont*
8	16	*La fête de Petit Pont*
	17	*Le jeu des questions*
1 – 8	18 – 25	Personal record sheets

Using the Domino puppet

Almost any exchange or dialogue with children in French (e.g. asking them which TV programmes they like) is an opportunity to use the Domino puppet. The advantages of doing this go beyond the obvious fun that is to be had.

- It is 'reasonable' for Domino to ask things that you yourself would not ask because you know the answers (e.g. a child's name);
- Many children will slip more readily into the role of play-acting if they can talk to Domino rather than to the teacher;
- There are many occasions too when children can be invited to manipulate Domino themselves, putting words into his mouth;
- By giving Domino a special voice you may feel less self-conscious about your own French accent!

En ville

Learning outcomes	Key language	Specific grammar and language awareness
• Saying where you are, asking where someone is • Saying where you are going, asking where someone is going • Asking and giving directions	• *Où est…? Il/ Elle est…* • *Où vas-tu? Je vais…* • *au, à la, à l'* • *Tourne à gauche/ à droite. Va tout droit.*	• the verb *aller*; the single word *vais* to translate "am going" • *au, à la, à l'* • affirmatives & negatives: *je veux/ ne veux pas; je peux/ ne peux pas*, etc. Flashcards 1 – 8

CD-ROM activities

1. Presentation of seven expressions of place using *au, à la, à l'*, and *sur le/ la*
2. Listen to short dialogues and click on the picture of the place referred to
3. Identify from a close-up where someone is, before the picture zooms out
4. Work out from a short animation which of five places you are heading to
5. Link 8 nouns to the right prepositional phrase: *au, à la* or *à l'*
6. Presentation of basic directions: *tourne à gauche/ à droite, va tout droit...*
7. Listen to a sentence and identify which of the spinning pictures goes with it
8. Follow directions to find a number of destinations
+ Speaking activity

How quickly or gently you launch into this unit will inevitably depend at which point in the school year you are beginning it. If it coincides with the start of a term, you may well wish to emphasise its revision potential. Either way, you will find that relatively little new vocabulary is introduced and that the topic of asking the way and giving directions provides a means of renewing children's familiarity with the geography of Petit Pont. Only a few things have changed (there is a petrol station, a new house, and at some distance beyond the town, a shopping centre) and these are best discovered, of course, through one of the virtual reality games on the CD-ROM.

Begin by asking children to **guess the meaning of the title** *En ville* (in town). If appropriate, **revise the names of places in Petit Pont**, using flashcards 6 – 12 from Petit Pont 1. Show two at a time and ask: *C'est la place ou la piscine?* etc. Children should then be ready to look at activity 1.

Page
1

1 Children have to **look at the six pictures and work out who is at each place**. This presupposes a certain familiarity with the characters and places in Petit Pont 1. Ask: *L'image a/ b/ c, qui est-ce?* ensuring they understand the meaning of *qui.*

13

Then break down the activity into steps:
1) Read the question.
2) Ask: *C'est quelle image, la piscine? C'est a, b, c, d, e ou f?*
3) Say: *Alors, qui est à la piscine?*

Answers:

à la piscine: Marie-Laure (e)

à l'école: Youssef (f)

au château: Domino (d)

au café: Céline (a)

sur le pont: Monsieur Moulin (c)

sur la place: Mathieu (b)

2 Begin by **revising the word *où***, asking a number of children the question: *Où habites-tu?*

The questions in this activity refer to the same pictures but they are turned round so children have to come up with the whole expression *à l'école, au château* etc. They will have heard these before but will not have been called upon to produce them. You could refer them for support to activity 1, where they appear in written form.

You may or may not want to include *Il est* or *Elle est* in the answers. If children are busy getting the places right, you could just add in these expressions when you repeat their answers, to help get them used to them. **Do not insist on whole sentence answers** just for the sake of it, but offer praise if some children do include *Il est* or *Elle est*. In any case, try to avoid children's repeating the people's names in their answers. It is unnatural in any language to answer the question "Where's Céline?" by saying "Céline's at the café."

Answers:

(Elle est) au café.

(Il est) sur la place.

(Il est) sur le pont.

(Il est) à l'école.

(Il est) au château.

(Elle est) à la piscine.

Use the **flashcards** again to **reinforce these expressions of place, emphasising the correct form of the preposition**. Hold up the café picture, make the Domino puppet pop up behind it, and ask: *Où est Domino?* to elicit *Au café,* and so on. Ask children to explain the meanings of the words *sur* and *à.* Then ask them what happens when the word *à* is followed by *la, l'* and *le.* This could be done as an investigative activity in pairs before bringing together their findings as a class. Ensure they understand that the one word *au* is the equivalent of the English "at the".

CD-ROM ACTIVITIES 1 – 3 reinforce these expressions.

3 CD TRACK 1

This activity is a vehicle for **revision** of the **personal questions** that were featured in Petit Pont 1. Their *raison d'être* is that here they are addressed to a child new to the school. Remember that **understanding the questions is as important as – if not more important than – understanding the answers**.

Write up on the board the following headings:

prénom:

âge:

frères et soeurs (+ prénoms):

anniversaire:

habite:

animaux:

couleur préférée:

Read through them to ensure children know their meaning. Then **encourage children to find the exact form of the questions** you would need to ask to find these things out, helping them where necessary. When they have all the questions, play the recording a first time, to let them get the general feel of the conversation and to recognise the questions they had themselves identified. Then play the recording a second time, pausing after each question and answer, and asking a volunteer to repeat the answer they heard. You can then write up, or ask a volunteer to write up, the information discovered about each topic.

14

Transcript:

Mathieu: *Comment tu t'appelles?*

Mélanie: *Mélanie.*

Céline: *Tu as quel âge?*

Mélanie: *J'ai neuf ans.*

Youssef: *Tu as des frères et soeurs?*

Mélanie: *J'ai un frère.*

Youssef: *Il s'appelle comment?*

Mélanie: *Il s'appelle Thomas.*

Marie-Laure: *C'est quand, ton anniversaire?*

Mélanie: *Le trente janvier.*

Amélie: *Où habites-tu?*

Mélanie: *A Petit Pont, rue du pont.*

Benoît: *Tu as un animal à la maison?*

Mélanie: *Oui, une tortue.*

Marie-Laure: *Quelle est ta couleur préférée?*

Mélanie: *Euh... le vert.*

Answers:

prénom: Mélanie

âge: 9 ans

frères et soeurs (+ prénoms): 1 frère, Thomas

anniversaire: le 30 janvier

habite: rue Pasteur, Petit Pont

animaux: une tortue

couleur préférée: le vert

End by asking children **questions in the third person** about Mélanie, with the answers on the board for them to refer to: *Il y a une nouvelle fille à l'école de Petit Pont. Elle s'appelle comment? Quel âge a-t-elle? Elle a des frères et soeurs? C'est quand, son anniversaire? Où habite-t-elle? Elle a des animaux à la maison? Quelle est sa couleur préférée?*

You could even remove or cover up the written answers and ask the questions again, in a different order, to see how much they can remember! This could be done as a team quiz.

Copymaster 1
La nouvelle fille

This consists of the eight questions asked of Mélanie which children have to match with her answers. The answers can be cut out and stuck in the correct place after each question.

Answers: *see transcript above.*

Page **2**

Introduce the **four new place names** using flashcards 1 – 4 (*le cinéma, le centre commercial, la rivière, la boulangerie*) drawing children's attention to the gender of each. Concerning pronunciation, encourage them as usual not to stress one syllable at the expense of another in these names, **every syllable carrying equal weight**. You can make this point most effectively by drawing the contrast with words that are similar to the English, like *cinéma, madame, Charlotte, conversations, activités* and *commercial*.

> The equal stressing of syllables in French is one of the things that makes it hard to untangle the individual words when you hear it spoken. It is difficult for a learner, for example, that the first two syllables of *à l'école* sound just like *aller*, or that in the sentence *Qui est au château*, because the *t* of *est* is run on, there are in fact two identical syllables: *tau* and *teau*. This is one reason why being familiar with the little words like *au* and *à la* is more than just a matter of grammatical accuracy: understanding them actually helps you to decode what you are hearing.

Play one or two **flashcard games** combining the **new place names** with those previously learned: Petit Pont 1 flashcards 6 – 13 and Petit Pont 2 flashcards 1 – 4. (See page 9 of the introduction for games ideas.)

In this activity children **listen to the dialogues**, identify where the people say they are, then **draw lines to link the people to the places**. Begin by looking together at the illustration and reading the speech bubbles. Ask a few pairs to act out the question and answer. Then read through the list of names and places. This will be the first time they have seen the written names of the new places.

Transcript:

Mélanie: *Bonjour, madame. Mathieu est là?*

Mme Duval: *Non, il est au stade.*

Youssef: *Benoît est là?*

Mme Abdouni: *Non, il est à l'école.*

Samia: *Salut. Amélie est là?*

Mathieu: *Non, elle est au cinéma.*

Marie-Laure: *Charlotte est là?*

Céline: *Non, elle est au centre commercial, avec maman.*

Une dame: *Bonjour. Madame Duval est là?*

Jean-Philippe: *Non, elle est à la boulangerie.*

Answers:

Mathieu — au cinéma
Benoît — à la boulangerie
Amélie — au stade
Charlotte — à l'école
Madame Duval — au centre commercial

The next stage is the **transition** from:
Où est Domino? Au stade.
to
Où vas-tu? Au stade.

In other words we are **replacing the verb être with the verb** *aller* **and the meaning of** *au* **changes from "at the" to "to the".**

Demonstrate the second question and answer using the Domino puppet and making him walk towards the picture of the sports ground. Repeat the question with different flashcards and encourage children to provide the answer. **Lead them towards noticing for themselves** that the expression of place (*au stade, etc.*) does not change as it would have to in English, where "at the..." would become "to the...".

Next, introduce the verb *Je vais* into the answers: *Où vas-tu? Je vais au stade.*

Continue, using this verb with various place names.

CD-ROM ACTIVITY 4 provides an ideal way of introducing the new forms *Où vas-tu?* and *Je vais...* in combination with the expressions of place.

The *Attention* feature in the book serves three purposes:
1 to reinforce the expressions *à la, à l'* and *au*
2 to underline the fact that these are the French for both "at the" and "to the".
3 to underline that *à + le* becomes *au*.

Write up *la boulangerie* on the board, then insert *à* before it. Do the same for *l'école*. Then write up *le stade*, but instead of writing *à* before it, rub out the *le* and insert *au*.

To practise this with the four new nouns, you could use the Domino puppet again, asking *Où va Domino?* as you hold up the flashcard of, say, the bakers and elicit the answer *Il va à la boulangerie*.

If you want to do more work on this language point, here are some ideas:

• Write in large letters on separate sheets of paper each of the twelve nouns as well as the three variants *au, à la* and *à l'*. Give each sheet to a different child, ensuring you allocate the latter three (*au, à la* and *à l'*) to children who understand the concept. Now hold up, or ask a child to hold up, one flashcard at a time. The two children with the appropriate words run to the front of the class and hold them up together to produce the correct phrase, e.g. *à la boulangerie*.

- To make this into a competitive game, divide the class into two teams and distribute identical sets of sheets to each team. The first team to display the correct phrase for a given flashcard wins a point.
- Start a phrase orally by saying *au, à la* or *à l'*, and either point to a child or ask for a volunteer who has to provide a compatible noun. Remember that they have only learned one phrase using *à l' (à l'école)*.
- Play the same game, but throwing a soft ball/ beanbag to a child as you say the starter. They must then say a noun that fits and throw it either back to you or, if they can supply a starter themselves, to another child in the circle.
- CD-ROM activity 5 also practises this grammar point.

2 This activity involves **finding the right answer to the question** *Où vas-tu?* to go with each of the five pictures. It can be done **orally, in writing, or both**. **A menu of answers** is provided in the book, so children do not need to have learned spellings in order to accomplish the task.

Answers:

a *(Je vais) à l'école.*

b *(Je vais) au centre commercial.*

c *(Je vais) à la rivière.*

d *(Je vais) à la maison.*

e *(Je vais) au stade.*

3 Children can now **invent and perform** their own conversations based on the expressions used in activities 1 and 2. Give an example of how these could be combined, illustrating it with the appropriate flashcards. Some children may find it helpful to see a written version on the board.

Bonjour. Céline est là?
Non. Elle est au café. Où vas-tu?
Je vais au cinéma.

Ask the rest of the class a question after each dialogue, to encourage them to listen to the detail, e.g. *Où est Céline? Où va Sam?*

CD TRACK 3

Song: Où vas-tu aujourd'hui?

Où vas-tu, aujourd'hui?
Je vais au stade.
Moi aussi!
Ah, c'est bien! Allons-y!
On y va ensemble.

Où vas-tu, aujourd'hui?
Je vais au café.
Moi aussi!
Ah, c'est bien! Allons-y!
On y va ensemble.

Où vas-tu, aujourd'hui?
Je vais au château.
Moi aussi!
Ah, c'est bien! Allons-y!
On y va ensemble.

This song consists of a **single repeated verse** in which **just the place name varies** each time (*au stade, au café, au château*). It introduces two more phrases using the verb *aller*: *allons-y* and *on y va*. These and other parts of the verb are summarised in the *Attention* feature that follows.

The song takes the form of a dialogue, so different halves of the class could take alternate lines, all singing the last line together:

A – *Où vas-tu, aujourd'hui?*
B – *Je vais au stade.*
A – *Moi aussi!*
B – *Ah, c'est bien! Allons-y!*
A+B – *On y va ensemble.*

Children may like to add verses using *au pont, à l'école*, or *à la place*. If so, allow them to discover for themselves that other longer expressions like *à la boulangerie* will not fit into the rhythm.

Attention
Read through this together, taking the opportunity to **revise *il* and *elle*.** Deal directly with the fact that there are **two words for "we"**: *on* and *nous*, and that the verb that goes with them is different for each. Remember that this is without a doubt one of the most useful verbs in the language (providing in addition the commonest way of talking about the future), so the value of learning these expressions by heart cannot be overstated.

4 This word stream can be untangled into **a three-line conversation**. Since it involves **copy writing**, it provides a fun way of focusing children's attention on the spelling of individual words without their actually having to memorise them. It also gives you the opportunity to reinforce the need for a capital letter at the beginning of a sentence, and of the conventions of punctuation common to both French and English.

> Answer:
>
> *Où vas-tu?*
>
> *Je vais à la rivière. Et toi?*
>
> *Moi, je vais à la maison.*

Page 4

The aerial view of Petit Pont sets the scene for **giving and understanding directions**. Introduce the three main directions first, then *Traverse le pont*, using flashcards 5 – 8 or activity 6 on the CD-ROM.

The similarity between *à droite* and *tout droit* is potentially confusing, so meet it head on, **emphasising that the 't' is heard** in *à droite* and getting children to practise pronouncing the two.

Practise these four instructions quickly using flashcard games (see p 00 of the introduction), CD-ROM activity 6, and *Domino dit* (like 'Simon says' in which children make an agreed gesture to go with the instruction only if it is preceded by the words *Domino dit*.). Bear in mind that some children may be very poor at the notion of left and right even in their own language.

Play *Où est le trésor?* or *Où est Domino?*, where a child is sent out of the room, an item representing *le trésor* or the Domino puppet is given to another child somewhere in the room who must keep it hidden, then the first child is called back in and a volunteer has to give them directions round the room to find the treasure or the dog. Before moving on, **introduce the word *puis*,** also printed in the book, demonstrating how it can be used to link two instructions, e.g. *Tourne à gauche puis va tout droit.*

1 CD TRACK 4

This consists of **four sets of directions** to places in Petit Pont, based on the starting point marked on the aerial view. Children have to **work out where they lead** to. Each set of directions is repeated twice. There is of course more than one possible answer to some of these. Before beginning, ensure all children are clear where exactly you are starting from.

Written versions of the key phrases are given in the book.

> **Transcript:**
>
> **1** *Tourne à droite, puis va tout droit.*
>
> *Tourne à droite, puis va tout droit.*
>
> **2** *Tourne à gauche.*
>
> *Tourne à gauche.*
>
> **3** *Tourne à droite, puis à gauche.*
>
> *Tourne à droite, puis à gauche.*
>
> **4** *Tourne à droite, va tout droit et traverse le pont.*
>
> *Tourne à droite, va tout droit et traverse le pont.*

> Answers:
>
> **1** *On va au café.*
>
> **2** *On va au stade/ à la piscine.*
>
> **3** *On va à l'école.*
>
> **4** *On va à la boulangerie/ à la place.*

2 Using the same starting point, **children** now **formulate the instructions** to get to four places named. If children ask how to say 'right again', you may like to introduce the phrase *encore à droite.*

Teach the expression *Pour aller.....?*, asking children the meaning of the word *aller* which appeared as a heading to the *Attention* summary on page 3, but which they will not previously have seen in a phrase.

> Answers:
>
> *Pour aller à l'école: Tourne à droite, puis à gauche.*
>
> *Pour aller au château: Tourne à droite, puis (encore) à droite (puis va tout droit).*
>
> *Pour aller à la place: Tourne à droite, va tout droit et traverse le pont.*
>
> *Pour aller au stade: Tourne à gauche, puis va tout droit.*

3 CD TRACK 5

Say: *A Petit Pont il y a quatre maisons marquées A, B, C et D.* (Point them out on the illustration) *Ecoute la conversation. Où habite Monsieur Moulin?* Repeat the instruction, with the appropriate name, for the second and subsequent dialogues.

> **Transcript:**
>
> 1 *Où est la maison de Monsieur Moulin, s'il te plaît?*
>
>   *Tourne à droite, va tout droit, traverse le pont, puis va tout droit.*
>
>   *Merci.*
>
>   *De rien.*
>
> 2 *Où est la maison de Marie-Laure, s'il te plaît?*
>
>   *Tourne à droite, puis à gauche et c'est tout droit.*
>
>   *Merci.*
>
> 3 *Où est la maison de Benoît, s'il te plaît?*
>
>   *De Benoît? Tourne à droite, traverse le pont, puis tourne à gauche.*
>
>   *Merci.*
>
>   *De rien.*
>
> 4 *Où est la maison de Youssef, s'il vous plaît?*
>
>   *Tourne à droite, puis encore à droite.*
>
>   *Ah, super. Merci.*
>
>   *De rien.*

Answers:

la maison de Monsieur Moulin = C

la maison de Marie-Laure = A

la maison de Benoît = D

la maison de Youssef = B

Copymaster 2
Plan de Petit Pont

Children can **colour in and label** this map of Petit Pont, using the names provided at the bottom of the sheet (the word *station service* is introduced here, a recent addition to the town). This will help familiarise them with the geography of the place, as will their playing any of the virtual reality games on the CD-ROM, in which they can navigate around the town at will.

Children can now try to **invent their own dialogues** in which one is asking the way of the other. This can either refer to the above copymaster or to their own hometown – or even to an imaginary place. In any case, model a sample dialogue with a pupil before handing over to pairwork.

Page
5

CD TRACK 6 Pronunciation

Ask children to **identify the sound** common to all six words (*our*). Emphasise the length of this sound, for which it is indispensable for the lips to be in a 'pouting' position.

> **Transcript:**
>
> *pour*
>
> *tourne*
>
> *jour*
>
> *aujourd'hui*
>
> *cour*
>
> *tour*

This is a good time to **play a game** in which you **say a French word** and children have to **find another one that rhymes with it**. Here are some examples:

pont	*maison, poisson, on, crayon, marron*
vert	*anniversaire, rivière, mère, père, Angleterre*
combien	*chien, bien, main, vingt*

gâteau	château, drapeau, cadeau, mot
commercial	animal, cheval, (pas) mal
chat	cinéma, chocolat, pas, ça va
oui	qui, lundi, mardi, etc.

🔘 CD TRACK 7 Poème

This poem is designed both to **reinforce negatives** and to **teach** the **useful classroom phrases** *Je ne peux pas and Je ne sais pas*. Children should learn and perform it with the actions and facial expressions indicated below.

🔘 CD TRACK 8 Story: Quelle coïncidence!

You can either **tell the story yourself**, using the script below, and clarifying its meaning with mime and gesture, or you can **play the recording** while children look at the illustrations in the book or on the interactive whiteboard. The story contains many of the key phrases from the unit.

On a second or third reading, children could act it out themselves.

J'aime.

Je n'aime pas.

Je veux.

Je ne veux pas.

Je sais.

Je ne sais pas.

Je peux.

Je ne peux pas.

Transcript:

Quelle coïncidence!

Un jour à Petit Pont, Marie-Laure va à la maison de Céline. Elle frappe à la porte. Toc toc toc! La maman de Céline ouvre la porte.

«Bonjour, madame,» dit Marie-Laure. «Est-ce que Céline est là, s'il vous plaît?»

«Non, Marie-Laure. Elle est au stade.»

«Ah, d'accord. Merci.»

Alors, Marie-Laure va au stade. Elle traverse le pont, elle va tout droit. Au stade elle trouve Youssef. Mais Céline n'est pas là.

«Où est Céline?» demande Marie-Laure.

«Elle est allée au café,» dit Youssef.

«Ah, d'accord. Merci.»

Alors, Marie-Laure va au café. Au café, elle trouve Mélanie et Charlotte. Mais Céline n'est pas là.

«Où est Céline?» demande Marie-Laure.

«Elle est allée à la rivière avec Domino,» dit Mélanie.

«Ah, d'accord. Merci.»

Alors, Marie-Laure va à la rivière. A la rivière elle trouve Benoît. Mais Céline n'est pas là.

«Où est Céline?» demande Marie-Laure.

«Elle est allée chez toi.» dit Benoît.

«Chez moi?» dit Marie-Laure. «Merci. Salut.»

Elle traverse le pont, elle tourne à droite, et elle va vite à la maison.

Et devant la maison elle trouve …. Céline et Domino.

«Ah! Te voilà!» dit Céline. «Tu étais où?»

«Euh… au stade, au café et à la rivière,» dit Marie-Laure.

«Eh bé, moi aussi!» dit Céline. «Quelle coïncidence!»

Unité 2 · Quel temps fait-il?

Learning outcomes	Key language	Specific grammar and language awareness
• Asking and saying what the weather is like • Compass directions • Saying which part of the country a place is in • The location of several famous sites in France	• *Quel temps fait-il?* • *Il fait beau/ gris/ chaud/ froid. Il pleut, il neige* • *Où se trouve…?* *Bordeaux se trouve…* • *au nord, au sud, à l'est, à l'ouest*	• *Il fait* + weather adjectives • Reading a text of up to 5 sentences Flashcards 9 – 15

CD-ROM activities

1 Presentation of six types of weather
2 Decide if the type of weather named matches the picture
3 Type in the missing weather word that describes each of four animations
4 Select graphics of the weather and the place referred to in eight recordings
5 Presentation of the points of the compass and the names of nine French towns
6 Identify which part of France (N, S, E or W) various towns are in
7 Unscramble sentences describing weather conditions in different parts of France
8 Follow instructions to find the treasure on a desert island
+ Speaking activity

Page 6

Begin by **asking the title question**: *Quel temps fait-il?* and looking and pointing out of the window. Then give a suitable answer from those on page 6, illustrating it with the appropriate flashcard (9-14) or a sketch on the board. **Ask children to repeat both question and answer** after you till they are pronouncing them well. Then introduce the other possible answers to the question orally, one at a time, using either the CD-ROM (activity 1) or flashcards 9 – 14. Teach the four expressions beginning *Il fait* first, before moving on to *Il pleut* and *Il neige*. This is an ideal context in which to **use different tones to say the phrases** e.g. happy, disappointed, surprised, grumpy, getting children to repeat them in the same tone of voice.

You can now **practise these using activity 2 on the CD-ROM** and/ or various games. In addition to one or two of the flashcard games suggested in

the introduction (p. 9), you could also play the following.

• One child mimes a reaction to a particular sort of weather (sweating, shivering etc.) and the others have to say what the weather is like.
• Agree a simple mime to accompany each type of weather. Then hold up one flashcard or say one weather expression at a time. Children have to do the appropriate mime to go with it. Speed up the game until they are barely able to keep up!

The written forms of the six types of weather are in the book. Depending on your approach, i.e. whether you think it is helpful for children to see the written word early in the learning process, you may wish to direct children to these either before doing the first listening activity, or after.

1 CD TRACK 9

This consists of ten short recordings, first **single statements**, then **short dialogues**, in which the **weather** is mentioned. Play the CD, pausing after each statement. Either **display the six flashcards** and ask a volunteer to come forward and point out the appropriate one, or **invite a volunteer to repeat the weather phrase** they have heard.

With very able children, ask them to write a word or draw a symbol to show the type of weather referred to, and check everyone's written answers at the end.

> **Transcript and Answers:**
>
> 1 *Regarde, Domino!* **Il fait beau!**
>
> 2 *Ah super!* **Il neige!**
>
> 3 *Oh là là! Qu'est-ce qu'**il fait chaud!**
>
> 4 **Il fait gris** *aujourd'hui. Regardez.*
>
> 5 *Ah non, c'est pas vrai!* **Il pleut!**
>
> 6 *Tu veux jouer au foot?*
>
> *Mais non.* **Il fait froid.**
>
> 7 *Quel temps fait-il?*
>
> **Il fait gris.**
>
> 8 *Quel temps fait-il là-bas?*
>
> **Ici il neige.**
>
> *Ah génial!*
>
> 9 *C'est bien.* **Il fait chaud** *ce matin.*
>
> *Oui, c'est bien pour le pique-nique.*
>
> 10 *C'est mon anniversaire et* **il pleut.**
>
> *C'est pas grave. On va aller au cinéma.*

Copymaster 3
Mon journal du temps

Children can now **make their own weather diary**. Following the example, they should write the day and date in the left column, and a description of the weather in the right hand column. You can either do this together, at least for the first few days, or leave children to fill it in on their own. Depending on the class, you may also want to subdivide each day into *matin* (morning) and *après-midi* (afternoon). They could also decorate the sheet. The completed diaries should make a good display.

2 Choosing an appropriate weather expression and one of the place names given, children **complete the short description** that accompanies each of the four pictures.

Finally, they could **draw a similar picture** of their own and **write two sentences** to describe it.

> **Answers:**
>
> *Il pleut. Mathieu va à la maison.*
>
> *Il fait gris. Céline va au stade.*
>
> *Il fait chaud/ beau. Benoît va à la rivière.*
>
> *Il neige. Marie-Laure va à l'école.*

CD-ROM ACTIVITY 4 practises this combination of weather and place in yet another way.

Page
7

Using **flashcard 15** or a drawing of your own, teach the French for the **four points of the compass orally**. You could identify the real compass points in relation to your classroom, then play a game in which you **point in a given direction** and children have to **call out its name in French**.

At this stage you could **introduce the written forms** of the words, using the compass in the book. Some children could **produce a sign** for

23

each of the compass points, which you could put up at appropriate points around the room.

Using a map of your own country or region, introduce the four expressions *au nord, au sud, à l'ouest, à l'est* by pointing to places and saying, for example: *Cardiff est au sud. Bangor est au nord.* Next, ask children to look at the **map of France showing the position of nine major towns**. Take time to practise pronouncing the names first.

CD-ROM activity 5 provides an alternative way of presenting them with native speaker pronunciation.

You may like to ask them if they know anything about any of the towns, or if any children want to volunteer to find out something about them for the class, using the internet. Then talk through the position of some of them, using the same four compass directions. Why not go one step further and introduce the phrases *C'est bon pour la santé* (It's good for you) and *C'est mauvais pour la santé* (It's not good for you)?

3 Children have to **supply the correct expression** (*au nord, au sud, à l'ouest, à l'est*) for each of four towns. You may want to do these orally before asking children to write them down.

> Answers:
>
> *Marseille est au sud.*
>
> *Calais est au nord.*
>
> *Strasbourg est à l'est.*
>
> *Bordeaux est à l'ouest.*

4 **Four more towns** for which they have to **find the right phrase**. This time the question is put directly, e.g. *Où est Paris?*

> Answers:
>
> *Toulouse: au sud.*
>
> *Nantes: à l'ouest.*
>
> *Lille: au nord.*
>
> *Grenoble: à l'est.*

To familiarise children with the names and positions of the compass points, as well as the relative locations of the named towns, play **a true/ false game**. Say a sentence such as *Bordeaux est au sud de la France.* Children

have to decide whether the statement is true or false. This can be done either with immediate responses (saying *vrai/ faux*, or by standing up if it's true), or by numbering your statements and asking everyone to write V or F each time and then going through the answers afterwards. If you opt for the latter, ensure you repeat the statements as you check them so children can see why they are right or wrong.

Children could play **a memory game based on the map**: in pairs, one child looks at the map and asks: *Où est Paris?* His/ her partner tries to reply from memory, without looking at the map. They then exchange roles.

CD-ROM activity 6 offers further practice on the same theme.

5 CD TRACK 10

This activity combines the names of the towns they have learned with the weather expressions. Begin by playing all the dialogues and asking children what they think they are about. This should elicit that the people are saying where they are and what the weather is like. Then replay one dialogue at a time, saying: *Ecoutez la conversation. Ils parlent de quelle ville: Paris, Marseille, Bordeaux? Quel temps fait-il?* To make it easier, deal with just the recognition of the town first, then play the recording again while they listen for the type of weather mentioned. When you have together identified that *Il fait beau à Marseille*, write up the name *Marseille* on the board and draw the sunny weather symbol next to it. Children can then be asked to **draw** this in, **in pencil**, on the map at the top of page 7.

You can then either work through the rest together, agreeing on the correct answers before they draw in the symbols, or you can let them draw in the symbols directly as they listen, checking their answers together afterwards. In either case, children should be allowed to hear the recordings at least twice before having to make up their minds.

> **Transcript:**
>
> – *Tu es où?*
>
> – *Je suis à Marseille.*
>
> – *Quel temps fait-il?*
>
> – *Il fait beau.*

- Tu es où?

- Je suis à Paris.

- Quel temps fait-il là-bas?

- Il fait froid.

- Allô.

- Salut. C'est moi, Benoît. Tu es à Bordeaux?

- Oui.

- Quel temps fait-il?

- Il pleut.

- Allô.

- Salut. Tu es où?

- Je suis à Toulouse.

- Il fait beau là-bas?

- Oui, il fait très beau.

- Vous êtes où?

- On est à Lille.

- A Lille!

- Oui.

- Quel temps fait-il?

- Il fait gris.

- Oui, ici aussi.

- Tu es où?

- Je suis à Grenoble.

- Ah super! Quel temps fait-il?

- Il neige.

- Vous êtes où?

- Nous sommes à Calais.

- Quel temps fait-il là-bas?

- Il pleut.

- Allô.

- Salut. C'est Marie-Laure. Tu es arrivée à Nantes?

- Oui.

- Quel temps fait-il là-bas?

- Il fait gris.

- Salut. Tu es où?

- Je suis à Strasbourg.

- Quel temps fait-il?

- Il fait froid.

Answers:

Marseille – sunny

Paris – cold

Bordeaux – raining

Toulouse – sunny

Lille – overcast

Grenoble – snow

Calais – raining

Nantes – overcast

Strasbourg – cold

Contre la montre

Read through the three questions, asking children what they mean. Encourage them to come up with an answer to the second one, using an appropriate expression, e.g. *au nord de l'Angleterre, à l'ouest du Pays de Galles*. The third one gives the opportunity to revise the French alphabet, by asking them to spell out the name of the place where they live. Get **two confident children to perform the dialogue** before asking **everyone else to practise it in pairs**. If children live in different places (with names of different lengths), ensure that the element of competition is only in relation to speeding up their own answers. As always, remember that **being able to ask the questions is as valuable as the ability to answer them!**

25

The five places shown in the photos are familiar to most French people. It is worth talking about them a little but this will clearly not be possible in French. Begin by asking children if they have heard of any of them and encourage them to say – or guess – whatever they can about them. To this you can add further information of your own:

The Eiffel Tower: built for the Great Exhibition of 1900 and originally intended to be dismantled afterwards, it soon became France's most famous monument and is now by far its most visited.

Mont Blanc: France's highest mountain, situated in the Alps, and also known for its glacier, which can be visited by cable car.

The Camargue: a flat area created by the Rhone delta, it is famous for its wild horses, its bird life (including flamingos) and its black bulls bred for bullfighting. On its edges are paddy fields where a considerable proportion of France's rice is grown.

The château de Chenonceaux: the Loire valley is the home of a number of France's most famous châteaux – more stately homes than castles – of which Chenonceaux is amongst the most spectacular.

Mont St Michel: an island off the West coast of Brittany which has been the home of Christian communities since the middle ages. Until a permanent road was built to it, it used to be cut off by the sea at every high tide. With its abbey perched at the top of its steep medieval streets, it is now one of France's favourite tourist destinations.

1   Children have to **copy the name of the right place into each gap**, based on the geographical descriptions given. More able children should enjoy working out the meanings of the sentences for themselves. For others, it will be worth seeing whether they remember what *se trouve* means, and asking them to guess the meaning of *la vallée* in the last sentence. Encourage everyone to be accurate in their copying.

> Answers:
>
> *Le Mont Blanc se trouve dans les Alpes.*
>
> *La Tour Eiffel se trouve à Paris.*
>
> *La Camargue se trouve au sud de la France.*

Le Mont St Michel se trouve à l'ouest de la France.

Le château de Chenonceaux se trouve dans la vallée de la Loire.

They could follow this up by **researching in pairs or groups other famous sites**, whether natural or historical: some children may have an interest in places themselves – from Le Mans famous for its 24-hour car rally to Bayeux famous for its tapestry, the West's first strip cartoon. If not, you could propose some names, but allow children to discover for themselves what they are famous for. Some possible ideas are: le Pont du Gard (Roman aqueduct near Marseille), Lascaux (with its world famous cave paintings), Avignon (with its unfinished half-bridge made famous by the song) or Millau (with the world's highest viaduct, opened in 2004). Their research on these could be made into a display, or used as the basis for presentations to the rest of the class or on computer.

2   Two texts – **a postcard and an email** from children on holiday. These are the longest pieces of writing they will have met in the book so far. Tackle one text at a time. It is important to **make clear from the start that they should not expect to be able to understand everything**. How you approach it will depend a great deal on the ability of individual children.

The most able will probably enjoy trying to understand it without help, looking up unfamiliar words and then tackling the questions in English on their own.

With others, you can ask them first to read it aloud in pairs (perhaps taking alternate sentences) and then tell each other anything they think they have understood. You can then go through it sentence by sentence, asking for suggested meanings. Be sure to focus on the things they have understood rather than the things they haven't. There is no virtue in avoiding English at this point. Working out what it means in English is what anyone but an excellent linguist is really doing in this situation, and there is no harm in confronting this honestly. **Ask children to give the gist of each sentence, guessing where necessary**.

Again, **guessing is an essential part of what anyone trying to operate in a foreign language** has to do. When you guess right, you are pleased, so children too who guess right should be given credit for it. If guessing doesn't work, ask them to look it up in the wordlist. They should then be ready to try and answer questions a – f about the postcard. With less able children you may prefer to do this together.

Use the same approach for the email but perhaps leaving them to work out a few more answers for themselves. They can then do questions g – j.

Answers:

a   *in the Alps*

b   *seven days*

c   *fine but cold*

d   *visit Mont Blanc, on Wednesday*

e   *he likes/ loves the snow*

f   *her class/ class CM1 at Petit Pont school*

g   *in Paris*

h   *five days*

i   *it's hot*

j   *visit the Eiffel Tower, today*

Finally, the texts contain some information that is not exploited in the questions. Rather than targeting this yourself, **ask children to invent a question or two** of their own that does not appear in the book (e.g. What sport is Céline doing? What does she say about it? Who did Youssef write to? Who is he staying with? In what part of Paris is he staying?) Other children could then try to answer them.

The school address

Point out the typically short address. In a town the size of Petit Pont, there would be no need to specify the street name for somewhere like the school, and the post code alone is enough to identify which part of France it is in: no region or *département* needs to be named.

You may like to explain that France is divided into 90 *départements*, numbered alphabetically, and that the first two numbers in any postcode

indicate the *département* (just as the *last* two on any vehicle number plate tell you which *département* it is from.)

The name of the class CM1 stands for *Cours Moyen 1* and is the equivalent of year 5 in England or P6 in Scotland. (Years 3 and 4 are called CE1 – *Cours élémentaire 1* – and CE2 and year 6 is CM2.)

By now children should know the texts fairly well. **Read each one out loud**, pausing at key points for them to try and remember the next word. Alternatively, read the text aloud while children follow it in their book. Stop at random points and ask someone to say the next word.

Providing the same text with gaps for children to complete (supplying a menu of the missing words if necessary) is another effective way of familiarising them with it. This can be done on the board, interactive whiteboard, using an OHP, or on computers.

3   Most children will need **structured support to write a postcard** of their own. There are different ways of providing this:

Reuse the text of the postcard in the book, replacing individual words to alter the meaning. Demonstrate this on the board or OHP. Differentiate by the number of words you suggest that children change. For example, some children could change just the names and three further details.

*Bonjour **Tom**!*
*Je passe **dix** jours dans les Alpes. Il fait **chaud**!*
J'adore le ski! Et Domino aussi aime la neige!
***Lundi** je vais visiter le Mont Blanc.*
Bisous
Darren

CD-ROM activity 7 offers practice in structuring sentences about the weather in different parts of the country.

Alternatively, use copymaster 4.

Copymaster 4
Carte postale

This provides **a 'kit' in the form of a menu of alternatives** from which children can put together a postcard text of their own. Read through it first together, eliciting as much of the meaning as possible and encouraging children to guess before providing the answers yourself.

The second part of the copymaster provides a 'kit' for writing a poem in which different place names rhyme with different types of weather. For more able children, the menu of written weather expressions could be removed using the Bookmaster programme, leaving children to produce the French themselves. The rhyming solution is:

A Paris, il fait gris.
A Bayeux, il pleut.
A Blois, il fait froid.
En Ariège, il neige.
A Chenonceau, il fait beau.

Page **10** 🔘 **CD TRACK 11 Pronunciation**

Ask children to identify the sound common to all six words (o/ eau/ au). After working on the sound itself, ask them to see how many different ways it is spelt in the words given.

Transcript:

stylo

photo

bientôt

Domino

beau

Bordeaux

château

beaucoup

au

chaud

gauche

aussi

🔘 **CD TRACK 12 Story: Le petit chat**

Tell or play the recording of the story as usual, using **mime and gesture** as well as the **illustrations** to support children's understanding. On a second reading, you could ask children to select the appropriate weather flashcard for each episode, and to write up the date named. Having

heard the story twice, they could be challenged to try and recall the four questions that Youssef asks the cat (*Ça va? Comment tu t'appelles? Où vas-tu? Où habites-tu?*).

Transcript:

Le petit chat

On est le mardi, vingt-trois septembre. Il fait chaud à Petit Pont. Youssef est sur le pont. Il voit un petit chat gris.

«Bonjour,» dit-il. «Ça va?»

Et le petit chat fait «Miaou.»

On est le vendredi, dix octobre. Il pleut à Petit Pont. Youssef va à l'école. Soudain, il voit le petit chat gris.

«Salut,» dit-il. «Comment tu t'appelles?»

Et le petit chat fait «Miaou.»

On est le dimanche, vingt-six octobre. Il fait beau à Petit Pont. Youssef est à la rivière. Soudain, il voit le petit chat gris.

«Salut, toi,» dit-il. «Où vas-tu?»

Et le petit chat fait «Miaou.»

On est le lundi, trois novembre. Il fait froid à Petit Pont. Youssef est à la maison.

Dans le jardin il voit le petit chat gris. Youssef ouvre la porte.

«Coucou,» dit-il. «Où habites-tu?»

Et le petit chat fait «Miaou.»

A ce moment, la maman de Youssef arrive.

«Ça va? Brrrr! Qu'il fait froid aujourd'hui! Oh, le pauvre petit chat!»

«Oui,» dit Youssef. «Il s'appelle Grisgris.»

«Ah?» dit sa maman. «Où habite-t-il?»

Et Youssef répond: «Il habite ici, chez nous.»

Quelle heure est-il?

Learning outcomes	Key language	Specific grammar and language awareness
• Asking and telling time on the hour • The words for the different parts of the day • Saying where someone is going and when	• *Quelle heure est-il?* • *Il est deux/ quatre heures.* • *le matin, l'après-midi, le soir* • *à sept heures*	• abbreviations 9h, 10h etc. • The 24-hour clock

CD-ROM activities
1 Presentation of times on the hour
2 Set a digital clock at given times
3 Identify the written time to go with the number of chimes you hear
4 Select the sentence in which the time of day mentioned best matches the picture
5 Choose the graphics that match what you hear to reveal successive parts of a picture
6 Multiple choice questions about a short animation
7 Match up ten questions and answers
8 Explore Petit Pont to find the opening times of various places
+ Speaking activity

The introduction of the topic **'telling the time'** is **limited in this unit to times on the hour**. Since children have already learned the numbers 1 to 12, they should be able to pick this up fairly quickly, but it is probably best to begin by briefly revising numbers anyway. Possible ways of doing this are:

• Throw a soft ball from one to the other with each child saying the next number in sequence.
• Allocate a number to each child, then call out a number randomly. The children with that number have to stand up.
• Write a number in the air for them to identify (remember to cross the sevens).
• Do some simple mental maths, e.g. *sept plus trois.*

Then, **using a clock face with moveable hands**, or CD-ROM activity 1, teach the hours orally starting with *une heure* and going up to *douze heures*. Ask the question *Quelle heure est-il?* each time, and get children to repeat this as well as the time itself. Draw attention to the liaison in *deux heures, trois heures, six heures* and *dix heures* and to the way the *x*'s and *s* effectively sound like a *z*. Point out too that the 'f' of *neuf* changes its sound to a 'v' in *neuf heures.*

You can then **play one or two games to practise** this:

• Children sit in circles of five to eight and take turns to say the hours in sequence. Like the clock, when they reach twelve they go back to one and start again.
• Make the game more fun by playing a variation on 'Buzz', using the idea of *un réveil* (an alarm clock) also introduced in activity 2 on the CD-ROM. Announce, for example, *Je mets le réveil à cinq heures,* illustrating this with the model clock. When it gets to the child whose turn it is to say *Il est cinq heures,* he or she makes a ringing noise instead. Periodically 'set' the alarm at a different time.
• Set the clock at a given hour and hold it up for everyone to see, saying a time as you do so, e.g. *Il est neuf heures.* If the time you say fits the time shown on the clock, children stand up or call out *Oui!* If it doesn't they remain seated or call out *Non!* Children who get it right could then take over your role setting the questions.

29

They can now **look at the written form**. Point them to the title of the unit first, then to the clock. Ask which English word they think is related to the French *heure*. See if they can work out why this word is spelt differently for just one of the times on the clock (no '*s*' on *une heure*). But be sure to emphasise that this '*s*' – as with other plurals – is silent. Ask why they think there are two words in the 'twelve' position and invite them to guess their meaning.

1 CD TRACK 13

Children **listen to the church clock of Petit Pont** striking the hour on eight different occasions and have to say what time it is.

> Answers:
>
> *Il est trois heures.*
>
> *Il est huit heures.*
>
> *Il est cinq heures.*
>
> *Il est douze heures/ midi/ minuit.*
>
> *Il est sept heures.*
>
> *Il est huit heures.*
>
> *Il est quatre heures.*
>
> *Il est onze heures.*

CD-ROM activity 3 reinforces the written form of different clock times.

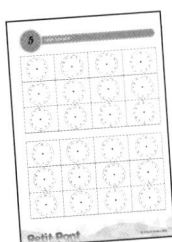

**Copymaster 5
Loto horaire**

This sheet provides two identical grids for playing **clock bingo**. Depending on how many times you want to play it, you can either give each child a whole sheet or cut them up and give them as many as you wish. First, tell children to **choose any clock and draw in the hands** at one o'clock, then choose another and draw in the hands at two, and so on up to twelve, until all the clocks show a different time on the hour. Then **play bingo by calling out different times**, being sure to repeat each one, with children putting a line through the corresponding clocks until they have a full horizontal row. They can then call out *«J'ai gagné!»* Ask them to name the four times in the completed row to confirm their win.

2 CD TRACK 14

This consists of five short dialogues, **each including a time**. Children should try to spot the time mentioned in each one, either writing down their answers or putting up their hands at the appropriate point as you recite the hours *une heure, deux heures* etc. after each dialogue (This gives everyone the chance to show what they think rather than just one child offering the answer).

Having established the times, you may like to play the recordings again, seeing how much children have understood (or guessed) about the context of each dialogue.

> **Transcript:**
>
> **1**
>
> *Quelle heure est-il?*
>
> *Cinq heures.*
>
> **2**
>
> *Hé, Youssef! Il est midi.*
>
> *Il est midi! D'accord. J'arrive!*
>
> **3**
>
> *Maman?*
>
> *Oui.*
>
> *Quelle heure est-il?*
>
> *Il est…. deux heures.*
>
> *Bon. Je vais au stade.*
>
> *D'accord.*
>
> **4**
>
> *Lève-toi, Youssef. Il est onze heures. Il fait beau.*
>
> **5**
>
> *Quelle heure est-il, Charlotte?*
>
> *Huit heures.*
>
> *Oh là là! C'est l'heure de Popstars!*
>
> *Ah oui!*

Answers:

1 *Il est cinq heures.*

2 *Il est midi/ douze heures.*

3 *Il est deux heures.*

4 *Il est onze heures.*

5 *Il est huit heures.*

3 This is an **open ended opportunity for children to try writing some times**. Based on the **visual clues**, they have to invent a realistic time for each picture. Since there are **no 'right' answers** except for the first picture, encourage different children to say what they have put.

Use the pictures in activity 3 to illustrate how children's answers could be developed by **referring to the time of day**. Introduce the expressions *du matin, de l'après-midi* and *du soir* by adding them to sample answers, e.g. (a) *Il est huit heures du matin.* (b) *Il est quatre heures de l'après-midi.* You could then look together at the three examples of their use in the book, at the top of page 12.

CD-ROM activity 4 focuses on their meaning by asking children to choose the appropriate expression for a series of pictures.

You may like to **point out that the terms a.m. and p.m. don't exist in French**. If you have access to other pictures illustrating different times of day, children could be asked to suggest times in French to match these.

Copymaster 6 Aujourd'hui

The copymaster consists of **six pictures showing people doing different things**, which correspond to six sentences. In each of the sentences a time is mentioned. By matching the sentences to the pictures, children have to **work out the time that goes with each picture** and fill in the hands on the clocks accordingly. With some children you may want to read through the sentences together first, or even match them to the pictures, before leaving them to fill in the times.

1 The three photos introduce some **real contexts** to the topic of telling the time, as well as **introducing the abbreviation 'h'** and how it is used between the hours and the minutes. They also give examples of **the 24-hour clock**, widely used in France for all official purposes. The shop sign with the miniature clocks provides an opportunity to talk about the long lunch break that is still an established part of French life. Look at the signs together, bearing in mind that some children may not be that confident about telling the time in their own language. Ask them to name the times in French. Then ask them to look at the four sentences a – d. You may need to **demonstrate the meaning of *ouvre* and *ferme*** if you have not already used these in relation to doors, windows or books. The **true/ false** task can be done either as a **class activity, in pairs, or individually**. In either of the last two cases, differentiate by identifying for some children which sentence goes with which photo, whilst leaving others to work this out for themselves.

Answers:

a *faux. Elle ouvre à six heures.*

b *vrai*

c *vrai*

d *faux. Elle est fermée le lundi.*

You could follow this activity up by **inventing together other sentences** about the opening times, or about those of local facilities, e.g. *Le parc ferme à.... La piscine ouvre à.....*

CD TRACK 15 Song: Il faut se dépêcher

The song introduces the **new phrases *Oh là là!*, *déjà*, and *il faut se dépêcher!* It can very effectively be accompanied by a series of gestures: looking at your watch (*Quelle heure est-il?*), panic (*Oh là là!*), and running on the spot for *il faut se dépêcher!* **Each verse repeats the same words** with just the hour changing. It is recorded right through to *minuit*, but you may wish to cut it short on some occasions! You may like to use the model clock to prompt children with the right time as the song progresses, or give children the opportunity to do this themselves.

Transcript:

Quelle heure est-il?

Oh là là!

Il est midi!

Midi déjà!

Il faut se dépêcher!

Quelle heure est-il?

Oh là là!

Il est une heure!

Une heure déjà!

Il faut se dépêcher!

Il est deux heures!

Il est trois heures!

etc.

Note that the expression *il faut* ('I/ you/ we must'), though often kept until later in French teaching, must be one of the commonest expressions in the language and, since it is invariable, is also one of the easiest to use. Use the phrase *Il faut se dépêcher!* in class whenever trying to hurry children along.

Page 13

This page is given over to a **pairwork game**: one child selects a set of related information (time, weather and destination). Their partner has to deduce the destination by asking questions about the time and the weather. The game provides **practice of asking as well as answering questions**, and also of thinking skills. Begin by going through all the **times**, then the **types of weather**, then the **destinations**, asking children themselves to produce the French for each one. Then read through the sample dialogue at the top of the page. Next, take the role of partner B yourself and invite a child to ask you the two questions *Quelle heure est-il?* and *Quel temps fait-il?* Finally, help them to deduce and tell you which place you are going to.

Children can then play the game in pairs, taking turns to be the questioner. They can play it over and over again, of course, and **the more they play it, the more confident they will become with the language** involved.

Page 14

The activities on this page serve the important purpose of **combining the language of this unit with vocabulary previously learned**. Most children should be able to tackle them on their own, or at least in pairs.

1 Find the **odd one out**. Encourage children to look up any words they have forgotten.

Answers:

a *à l'école*

b *vert*

c *temps*

d *chaud*

e *cheval*

f *heure*

2 The seven answers to this **crossword** are all key words from the first three units. The hidden word *mauvais* is new vocabulary. Illustrate its meaning through examples, e.g. *Aujourd'hui il fait froid et il pleut. Il fait mauvais.* Ask children to find a translation for it. Encourage them to use this new phrase in their weather diaries.

Solution

1		t	e	m	p	s
2		c	h	a	u	d
3			o	u	e	s	t
4				v	a	s
5		b	e	a	u
6	f	r	o	i	d
7			e	s	t

CD-ROM activity 6 offers further revision of the language of units 1 to 3, while activity 7 combines questions and answers from these with others from *Petit Pont 1*.

CD TRACK 16 Poème

This poem introduces the idea that it can be **one time in one place and another time in another**, and thus provides an opportunity for pointing out that France is permanently one hour ahead of Great Britain. Almost all its vocabulary should be familiar to children, apart from the colloquial *C'est pas facile.* They may need reminding of the verb *se trouve* which they first met in unit 2 when talking about the geographical position of places, e.g. *Marseille se trouve au sud.* Read through it together to begin with, then let them hear the recorded version before saying it in unison.

With its **repeated first three lines**, it is a prime candidate for **learning by heart**.

Having introduced the idea of time differences, play a game in which you say: *Il est neuf heures à (Newcastle). Quelle heure est-il à Paris?*

At different times of the day, point to the classroom clock if you have one and ask: *Quelle heure est-il en France?*

With more able children you may like to discuss the concept of time zones and – using the time difference quoted in the poem – may even ask them, for instance: *Il est dix heures à New York. Quelle heure est-il à Moscou?*

> **Transcript:**
>
> *Poème*
>
> *Quelle heure est-il?*
> *C'est pas facile,*
> *Quand on se trouve ici.*
> *Sept heures à New York,*
> *Trois heures à Moscou,*
> *Et midi à Paris!*
>
> *Quelle heure est-il?*
> *C'est pas facile,*
> *Quand on se trouve ici.*
> *Est-ce le matin?*
> *Ou est-ce le soir?*
> *Ou est-ce l'après-midi?*

Page 15

CD TRACK 17 Pronunciation

Ask children to **identify the sound** common to the words listed (*ou*). Point out the part it plays – not obvious at first – in the word *oui.* Having practised the sound, making a large a hollow of their mouths as they can, challenge children to think of other words they know which contain it. Possibilities include *trousse, douze, rouge, Toulouse, couleur, route* and *épouvantail.*

> **Transcript:**
>
> *où, écoute, ouest, trouve, oui, tout, vous, boulangerie, ouvre, beaucoup*

CD TRACK 18 Story: Qu'est-ce qu'il y a, Domino?

The phrase of the title should be familiar to children from the various versions of the main Petit Pont song, but here it takes on a new meaning: **'What's wrong?'** or **'What's the matter?'** As usual, you can either tell the story yourself using the text below, or play the recording of it. Use expression and gesture to clarify the meaning of such new phrases as *à toute à l'heure* (see you soon), *personne ne comprend* (nobody understands), *Céline dort* (Céline is asleep), and *pauvre Domino!* (poor Domino!)

On a subsequent telling or playing, a child could be asked to set the clock at the appropriate hour for each episode. This story lends itself well to being acted out, with children taking the parts of Mum, Dad, Céline and Domino.

> **Transcript:**
>
> Qu'est-ce qu'il y a, Domino?
>
> *C'est un jeudi. Il est huit heures du matin. Domino est dans son panier. Céline va aller à l'école.*
>
> *«Bonne journée,» dit maman.*
>
> *«Merci,» dit Céline. «A toute à l'heure.»*
>
> *Soudain, Domino aboie. «Ouah! Ouah!»*
>
> *Qu'est-ce qu'il y a, Domino? dit Céline.*
>
> *«Ouah! Ouah!» répète Domino.*
>
> *Mais personne ne comprend.*

33

Il est quatre heures de l'après-midi. Céline rentre de l'école.

«Bonjour, maman,» dit-elle. «Bonjour, Domino.»

Soudain, Domino aboie. «Ouah! Ouah! Ouah! Ouah!»

Qu'est-ce qu'il y a, Domino? dit Céline. «Tu as faim?»

«Ouah! Ouah!» répète Domino.

Mais personne ne comprend.

Il est onze heures du soir à Petit Pont. Céline dort. Charlotte aussi.

Soudain, Domino aboie. «Ouah! Ouah! Ouah! Ouah!»

«Qu'est-ce qu'il y a?» dit maman.

Mais Domino continue: «Ouah! Ouah! Ouah! Ouah!»

«Qu'est-ce qu'il y a, Domino?» dit Céline. «Il y a un fantôme?»

«Mais non!» dit papa. «Il n'y a pas de fantôme.»

«Ouah! Ouah!» répète Domino.

Mais personne ne comprend.

Le lendemain, papa se lève. Il est sept heures du matin.

«Où est mon portable?» dit-il?

«Il n'est pas dans ton pantalon?» dit maman.

«Non.»

«Il n'est pas dans ton sac?» dit maman.

«Non.»

Soudain, Domino aboie. «Ouah! Ouah! Ouah! Ouah!»

«Qu'est-ce qu'il y a?» dit maman.

Mais Domino continue: «Ouah! Ouah! Ouah! Ouah!»

Maman regarde dans son panier. Et voilà le portable de papa! – le portable qui est sur silencieux et qui vibre – Vrrrrr! Vrrrrr! – dans le panier.

«Ah! C'est pour ça que Domino aboyait!»

«Pauvre Domino!» dit maman.

«Merci, Domino!» dit papa.

Le corps humain

This two page section introduces the vocabulary of the human body. Do not start with the book straight away, but rather teach the eight words featured on page 16 orally through a combination of routines and games. Begin by pointing to the parts of your body as you name them one at a time: *la tête, les oreilles, les yeux, le nez, la bouche, les mains, le ventre, les pieds*. Children should repeat them after you, pointing at the appropriate parts of themselves. Change the order as you carry on, then say the words but pause before pointing so children have the chance to show if they know their meaning. Next, point to something and let children supply its name.

You can always add further words later if you want to, but sticking to these to begin with will make the action rhyme simpler and more effective.

Page 16

CD TRACK 19 Rime

The rhyme should be spoken rhythmically, touching the appropriate parts of the body (which go from top to toe). If you want to sing it, it fits the tune of "Heads, and shoulders, knees and toes" very neatly!

> **Transcript:**
>
> *La tête, les oreilles, les yeux, le nez.*
>
> *La bouche, les mains, le ventre, les pieds.*

1 Children can then **draw in lines to link the labels to the right parts of the body** on the picture of Mathieu.

Page 17

2 This exercise **reminds children that the words for parts of the body**, like all other nouns, **are either masculine or feminine**. In order to discover which, they can refer to page 16 in some cases (*la bouche, le nez, le ventre, la tête*), but for the words they have met in the plural (*les mains, les pieds*) they will have either to look it up, or to be told. Discuss this with them to help **consolidate their understanding of the concept**, which is arguably more important at this stage than their actually knowing the correct gender for particular nouns.

Answers:	
le nez	*la bouche*
le ventre	*la tête*
le pied	*la main*

3 **Revising the words for colours**, this activity involves colouring in the parts of the scarecrow according to the description. Children have met all the vocabulary before but you may want to read through it first. Invite them to guess the meaning of the word *reste*.

This rap should be accompanied by **actions** as illustrated next to the song. It involves children closing and opening their eyes whilst singing and requires a considerable amount of concentration, thereby generating a lot of fun. A gesture with each hand can accompany the words *"Un, deux"*.

> **Transcript:**
>
> *Un, deux.*
> *Un, deux.*
> *Touche ta bouche.*
> *Ferme les yeux.*
>
> *Un, deux.*
> *Un, deux.*
> *Touche ta tête.*
> *Ouvre les yeux.*
>
> *Un, deux.*
> *Un, deux.*
> *Touche ton nez.*
> *Ferme les yeux.*
>
> *Un, deux.*
> *Un, deux.*
> *Touche tes oreilles.*
> *Ouvre les yeux.*
>
> *Un, deux.*
> *Un, deux.*
> *Touche tes pieds.*
> *Ferme les yeux.*
>
> *Un, deux.*
> *Un, deux.*
> *Touche ton ventre.*
> *Ouvre les yeux.*

le/la/les or ton/ta/tes

When should you use *le/ la/ les* and when should you use *ton/ ta/ tes* with parts of the body?
Note that the instructions referring to actions that you can only do to yourself (opening or closing your eyes) use the word *les*, precisely because it's considered obvious whose eyes you are talking about. With the other instructions about touching parts of the body ("touch your head", "touch your feet", etc) the possessive pronoun *ton*, *ta* or *tes* is used, because you could be touching somebody else's.

You can now **play *'Domino dit'*** (like 'Simon says') using the same phrases. Children carry out the commands only if these are preceded by the words *Domino dit*. Although this is traditionally a competitive game, they do not necessarily have to drop out if they get it wrong.

Activities 4 and 5 in Unit 4 of the CD-ROM provide revision and practice on parts of the body.

Temps libre

Learning outcomes	Key language	Specific grammar and language awareness
• Sports and leisure activities	• *Je joue/ tu joues au basket/ foot...*	• prepositions after jouer (*au*) and faire (*du/ de la*)
• Asking and answering what sports people do	• *Je fais/ tu fais du vélo/ de la danse...*	• using the 24 hour clock
• Clock times with quarter past, half past and quarter to	• *... et quart, ... et demie, ... moins le quart*	• *oui* becoming *si* after a negative
• Clock times to the nearest five minutes	• *Non! Si!*	Flashcards 16 – 23
• Saying what time a TV programme is on		
• Saying what your favourite programme is		

CD-ROM activities
1 Presentation of seven sports or leisure activities
2 Click on the picture that goes with the sentences you hear
3 Type in the name of the activity to reveal its full picture
4 Presentation of parts of the body
5 Follow the instructions to colour in a picture of a clown
6 Match the written times to the correct clock
7 Trigger an animation by identifying the time you hear (includes quarter to/ past and half past intervals)
8 Decide whether a series of statements about a sports centre timetable are true or false
+ Speaking activity

This unit introduces the **names of some common sports and leisure pursuits**, and extends **telling the time to include minutes**. Begin by teaching the names of the seven sports activities using flashcards 16-22 and/or the CD-ROM activity.

All but the words *vélo* and *natation* are close to the English, so should present little difficulty, but take advantage of this to **insist on good pronunciation** as well as on the correct use of *le* and *la*. Note that the first five are masculine and the last three feminine.

Practise the new vocabulary orally using one or two flashcard games (see the introduction, page 9) or CD-ROM activity 2.

Once they are confident with the sound of these words, you can draw attention to their written form on the screen or in the book.

1 **Two important verbs** are needed when talking about leisure activities and sports: *jouer* and *faire*. It may be unfortunate that they link up to the nouns using different words (*au*, *du* and *de la*), but to avoid these expressions because of the potential difficulty would be to do children a disservice. What you can avoid is making too much of the grammatical detail so that, whilst reinforcing the correct usage, you are mainly congratulating children for communicating the intended meaning. They will not feel burdened by the underlying grammar so long as you do not let it become an obstacle to their expressing themselves.

Read through the eight questions together, with children repeating them after you. Then look at the three alternative answers: *oui*, *non* and *un peu*. Begin by asking individual children about the different activities, mixing questions with *Tu joues* and *Tu fais*, then hand it over to them to continue the interviews in pairs.

After a little while, interrupt the activity to ask one or two about their partners, e.g. *Sophie joue au tennis? William fait de la gymnastique?* The chances are they may not have paid much attention to their partner's answers, and the prospect of being asked about it should make them listen more carefully while they continue the pairwork.

Play the following game: **name a child and hold up a sports flashcard**. The child named has to name someone else and ask them whether they do that activity, e.g. *Robbie, tu joues au foot?* Then show another flashcard which that child has to ask someone else about, e.g. *Kerry, tu joues au tennis?* After a while they can continue the activity without being prompted by flashcards, choosing the sport themselves.

Next, extend the topic by **talking about what day they do these activities**. The best way of introducing this is to say what you do yourself, e.g. *Moi, je joue au tennis le samedi.* At this point you may need to **revise the days of the week**, saying them in sequence round the class. Ask two or three children to name the days when they do the sports they say they like, introducing the question *Tu fais ça quel jour?* and prompting them if necessary by adding *Lundi? Mardi?* Before expecting the majority of children to handle this language actively, move on to the following listening activity.

2 CD TRACK 21

Four of the Petit Pont **characters say a) what they like doing and b) which day or days they do it**. Children should listen to the recordings and draw in lines (in pencil!) to link together one item from each column. Be sure to let them hear each dialogue several times and repeat the key language if you wish before they draw in their lines.

It will depend on your class whether or not you wish, having completed the task, to draw attention to the use of *le* with the days of the week: *le mardi* meaning "on Tuesdays" or "every Tuesday", as opposed to simply *mardi*, meaning "on Tuesday"

> **Transcript:**
>
> **1** *Tu fais de la danse, Marie-Laure?*
>
> *Oui, j'adore ça!*
>
> *Tu en fais quand?*
>
> *Le jeudi.*
>
> **2** *Tu joues au foot, Mathieu?*
>
> *Oui, le mercredi et le samedi.*
>
> **3** *Tu joues au basket, Youssef?*
>
> *Oui. Je joue au basket le mardi et le vendredi.*
>
> **4** *Tu joues au tennis, Céline?*
>
> *Oui, c'est mon sport préféré.*
>
> *Tu fais ça quel jour?*
>
> [*Le mercredi.*

Answers:

Marie-Laure

Mathieu

Youssef

Céline

lun	
mar	
mer	
jeu	
ven	
sam	
dim	

lun	
mar	
mer	
jeu	
ven	
sam	
dim	

lun	
mar	
mer	
jeu	
ven	
sam	
dim	

lun	
mar	
mer	
jeu	
ven	
sam	
dim	

Sports in France

In France as elsewhere, sport is a compulsory part of the school timetable. However, there are very rarely any after school sporting activities. Children who are keen on a particular sport normally do this in a club that is quite independent of their school. Such clubs are heavily subsidised by the state, so membership is extremely cheap. Even very small towns generally have good sports facilities. Typically, primary aged children in a football club will get a training session once a week and will play weekly matches against other local clubs at weekends throughout the season. Particularly promising children will be given the opportunity to train and play at higher levels. This unitary national structure is probably the reason why France produces so many top players in a wide range of sports.

Since children have already learned and used the question *Tu aimes...?* in different contexts, together with a range of possible answers to it (*Oui. Non. Ça va.*), you should be able to move on quite quickly to allow them to express their

opinions about these same sports. Having asked a few children from the front (*Tu aimes la danse?* etc.), hand over to them to continue briefly in pairs. From this, they can move on to doing a survey using copymaster 7.

Use of le/ la/ les after Tu aimes...?

This can be developed as a habit rather than needing to be presented explicitly as a point of grammar. If you introduce it enough in different contexts, children will get used to hearing and using it themselves when talking about likes and dislikes: *Tu aimes le rouge/ la télé/ les chiens/ les bonbons?*

Copymaster 7
Sondage sur les sports

Tell children they are going to **carry out a survey**, asking other people whether they like each of the eight sports. (The blank rows at the bottom are there in case you want to introduce any additional sports that are popular with the class.) Carry out a few sample questions and answers, demonstrating how to put a tick in the appropriate column on the sheet. The speech bubbles at the top are there to remind them of the language to use. Children can work at their own speed – it doesn't matter how many interviewees they get through. When you bring the activity to a stop, they can then (with help if necessary) complete the sentence at the bottom of the sheet *Le sport préféré est le/ la....*

Activity 3 on the CD-ROM will motivate children to **spell correctly** the names of **five of the sports**.

Page
19

This page develops the topic of **telling the time**, so far restricted to times on the hour. Introduce **quarter past, half past and quarter to** using a clock face and/ or the illustrations in the book. Present a number of examples of each one before moving on to the next, with children repeating them after you.

Practise these using some of the games suggested at the beginning of unit 3 (see page 29).

Some children will find that seeing the written version helps them to distinguish the similar sounding *et quart* and *moins le quart*. Point out the **silent final 't'** on *quart*, as well as the **hard 'k'** sound of the *qu.* You could ask children to think of other words that begin with these letters (*quatre, quarante, qui, que, quand)*.

3 Six clocks on which children have to **draw in the hands** to match the written times. Make sure they do this in pencil so they can change their minds!

Further practice of half past and quarter to/ past is available in CD-ROM activities 6 and 7.

4 **CD TRACK 22** Quelle heure est-il?

This is a simple but enjoyable game in which you repeatedly show the class a clock with different times on it (on the hour, quarter past, half past or quarter to) and they have to say the time. But whenever it is a time on the hour they shout it out loud, **using the expression *pile*, meaning "on the dot"**, which rhymes of course with the question *Quelle heure est-il?* Begin by introducing the word *pile* and giving a couple of examples. Then play the recording so children can hear what is expected.

Transcript:

Quelle heure est-il?

Midi et demie.

Quelle heure est-il?

Trois heures et quart.

Quelle heure est-il?

Sept heures pile!

First, **revise the numbers** 5, 10, 15, 20, 25, 30 and 35. Then revise *quarante* and *cinquante*, emphasising their connection with *quatre* and *cinq*. It is important that children are comfortable with all these numbers before moving on to incorporate them into times.

Next, ask children for the other way in English of saying "quarter past five", "half past six" and "quarter to eight". Tell them that there are the same two ways of saying these in French as well.

Now present them with a time in French, e.g. *deux heures quinze,* and invite someone to set the clock to it. Do the same for *deux heures trente,* then *deux heures quarante-cinq,* asking each time for the other way of saying them, using *et quart, et demie* and *moins le quart*. Depending how quickly children grasp this, you can then show them a full five-minute series starting with *huit heures cinq* and moving the number of minutes up by five at a time till you reach *huit heures cinquante-cinq* and eventually *neuf heures*, encouraging *them* to name the times. Remember: all this is **reinforcing their concept of time** as well as teaching them French.

1 Ask children to **link up the written times** to the right clock face.

Answers:

a *trois heures dix*

b *cinq heures quarante*

c *sept heures vingt*

d *onze heures quarante-cinq*

e *une heure vingt-cinq*

f *quatre heures cinquante*

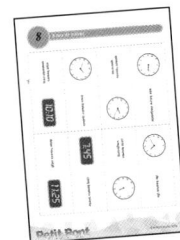

**Copymaster 8
Jeu de paires**

This is a set of word and picture cards based on **clock times**. Children cut them up and play pairs. They can also be stuck on paper or into their books as a matching exercise.

The **extract from the TV listings** puts clock times into a realistic context. It also confronts the issue of the twenty-four hour clock, commonplace in France. Some teachers may want to avoid this. In any case, if children are unsure about it, you will need to spend time explaining it. Read through the TV listings together, encouraging them to say the programme times in French (excellent practice of numbers! e.g. *quinze heures trente*) and to guess the meaning of any unfamiliar vocabulary.

Next, say one of the times and ask them to name the programme. They could come back to this and do it as pairwork after they have done activities 2 and 3.

2 Four sentences about the TV programmes for children to complete with a time in numbers. **The use of *à* with times** is introduced here. Draw children's attention to this when looking at the example (*Le journal est à vingt heures.*) Note that, when checking or agreeing answers orally, they will have to provide the word *heures* themselves.

    a *Le film est à 20.50.*

    b *Le match de foot est à 15.30.*

    c *Star Academy est à 18.10.*

    d *Qui veut être millionnaire? est à 19.00.*

3 Four **true/ false questions about the TV timings**. Before asking children to answer these, ask them to look at the sentences and see whether they notice anything about the times (The twenty-four hour times are rephrased in terms of the twelve-hour clock, e.g. 17.20 is called *cinq heures vingt.*). In this way the activity is not quite as obvious as it seems. You may also want to invite children to guess – or ask them to look up – the meaning of *jeu télévisé* (a game show).

> Answers:
>
> **a** *vrai*
>
> **b** *vrai*
>
> **c** *faux*
>
> **d** *vrai*

💿 **CD TRACK 23**

Children listen to **extracts of sound recordings from five of the programmes** and have to say for each one which programme they think it is. Before doing the activity, introduce the word *émission*, by saying: *Friends, le journal, le documentaire, sont des émissions* and inviting children to guess its meaning. Then tell them:

Ecoute. C'est quelle émission? and play the first extract.

> Answers:
>
> **1** *Star Academy*
>
> **2** *Documentaire: animaux d'Australie*
>
> **3** *Foot*
>
> **4** *la météo*
>
> **5** *Friends*

Page
21

4 Move straight on to asking whether children like particular programmes, reintroducing the expression *Tu aimes...?* Next, ask them *Quelle est ton émission préférée?* and follow this up by asking *C'est quel jour?* When these questions and answers have become familiar, children can write their answers to the written questions in the book.

💿 **5 CD TRACK 24**

Four of the *Petit Pont* **characters give the day and time of their favourite television programme**. Look at the names of the programmes first, explaining roughly what they are (*Smallville* is a popular drama series; *Les Minikeums* is a variation on the Muppets; *Le maillon faible* is The Weakest Link). Children then listen to what each person says and write in the day and time on the grid in the book. Alternatively, you may wish to do this listening activity as a class and then fill in the grid together. The times are expressed in a mixture of 12- and 24-hour clocks, as they would most likely be in real life. When you get to the last example, ask children to guess the meaning of the phrase *tous les jours.*

> *Céline, quelle est ton émission préférée?*
>
> *Mon émission préférée? Smallville.*
>
> *C'est quel jour?*
>
> *C'est le vendredi.*
>
> *A quelle heure?*
>
> *A dix-huit heures.*
>
> *Mathieu, quelle est ton émission préférée?*

Euh... les Minikeums.

C'est quel jour?

Le dimanche.

A quelle heure?

A neuf heures du matin.

Marie-Laure, quelle est ton émission préférée?

Star Academy.

C'est quel jour, Star Academy?

C'est le samedi.

A quelle heure?

A huit heures du soir.

Benoît, quelle est ton émission préférée?

le maillon faible.

C'est quel jour?

C'est tous les jours.

A quelle heure?

A seize heures.

Answers:

Prénom	Émission préférée	jour	Heure
Céline	Smallville	le vendredi	18.00
Mathieu	Les Minikeums	le dimanche	9.00
Marie-Laure	Star Academy	le samedi	8.00/ 20.00
Benoît	Le maillon faible	Tous les jours	16.00

Below the grid, children can fill in their own answer to the question: *A quelle heure est ton émission préférée?*

6 A **role play based on a disagreement about which TV programme to watch**. Children should **enjoy acting this out** convincingly and making it sound realistic. Read through the dialogue, pointing out the word *si* meaning "yes, I am" or "yes, I do". Explain that you can't answer *non* with *oui*. Introduced as a chant in this context, they should have no difficulty remembering this rule. The end of the dialogue can go on, of course, as long as they like!

CD TRACK 25 Pronunciation

Children should easily be able to identify that the **sound common to these words is *i***, pronounced like the vowel in "me" but with the sound being produced towards the front of the mouth rather than in the throat. Spend a moment to look at the spelling of *oui*, which children tend to liken to "we" but which in fact consists not of a consonant and a vowel but of two vowel sounds *ou* and *i*. It's only the transition from one to the other that produces the 'w' sound. Check that they remember what the words mean. You can then invite them to think of other words that contain the same sound (*Céline, facile, qui, six, tennis, rugby, rivière, ici...*).

> **Transcript:**
>
> *midi, film, il, demie, oui, millionnaire, si, émission, pile, gymnastique*

CD TRACK 26 Poème

This little **poem links a couple of weather phrases with the idea of watching television**. It is short enough to be **learned by heart**. Some children could be given the choice of which verse to learn. Alternatively, it could be performed by pairs as indicated in the transcript below. Point out the use of *on* meaning "we" and the four uses of the verb *fait*, which could not be translated by the same word in English. It is worth drawing children's attention to the spelling of the syllables that rhyme (*mauvais – fait – télé* and *froid – pas*) to underline that there are different ways of spelling the same sound.

Transcript and answers:

- *Tu as un animal, Benoît?*
- *Oui, j'ai deux chats.*

- *Quel âge as-tu, Marie-Laure?*
- *J'ai dix ans.*

- *C'est quand, ton anniversaire?*
- *C'est le onze février.*

- *Tu aimes la danse?*
- *Oui. J'adore ça.*

- *Quel temps fait–il?*
- *Il fait mauvais.*

- *Où habites-tu?*
- *A Petit Pont.*

- *Tu as des frères et soeurs?*
- *J'ai deux frères.*

- *Comment t'appelles-tu?*
- *Nicolas.*

- *Quelle heure est-il?*
- *Onze heures et demie.*

- *Quelle est ta couleur préférée?*
- *Le bleu.*

Page **22** 1 **CD TRACK 27**

This matching activity **revises** some of the **key questions and answers** learned so far. It can either be done as a reading task (preferable though more demanding), in which case children have to work out the meaning and the matches themselves, or as a listening task, in which case you will need to pause the recording after each question and answer. If you set it as a reading task, you may want to read the sentences aloud first, to aid recognition. When children have completed it, the recording can then be used to check the answers.

CD TRACK 28 Story: Problèmes de télé

This story reinforces the **language of telling the time** as well as the **phrases *Mais non! Mais si!***

As usual, you can either tell the story yourself using the text below, or play the recording of it. In either case, children can follow the pictures in the book or on the whiteboard CD-ROM. Use gesture to convey the meaning of *claque la porte* ("slams the door").

This story too is fun to act out, with someone changing the clock to the appropriate time for each episode.

Transcript:

Problèmes de télé

Il est lundi. Marie-Laure est à la maison.

«Quelle heure est-il?» demande-t-elle à Jean-Philippe.

«Six heures et quart,» dit Jean-Philippe.

«Ah super!» dit Marie-Laure. «Je vais regarder Star Academy.»

«Mais non!» dit son frère. «Je regarde ma série!»

«Ah non!»

«Mais si!»

«Mais non!»

«Mais si!»

Et Marie-Laure claque la porte et va chez Céline.

«Salut!» dit-elle. «Tu regardes Star Academy?»

«Non. La télé est en panne.»

«Ah non!»

«Mais si.»

«Quelle heure est-il?» demande Marie-Laure.

«Six heures vingt-cinq,» dit Céline.

«Allez,» dit Marie-Laure. «On va chez Benoît.»

Les deux filles arrivent à la maison de Benoît.

«Est-ce qu'on peut regarder Star Academy?» demande Céline.

«Non,» dit Benoît. «Mon père regarde le journal.»

«Ah non! C'est pas possible!» dit Marie-Laure.

«Mais si,» dit Benoît. «Allez chez Mathieu.»

«Quelle heure est-il?» demande Marie-Laure.

«Six heures trente-cinq,» dit Céline.

Alors Céline et Marie-Laure traversent le pont et vont chez Mathieu.

Mathieu est dans son jardin.

«Tu ne regardes pas Star Academy?» dit Marie-Laure.

«Mais non,» dit Mathieu. «Ce n'est pas aujourd'hui, Star Academy.»

«Mais si!» dit Marie-Laure.

«Mais non.»

«Mais si!»

«Mais non!» dit Mathieu. «Aujourd'hui on est vendredi. Star Academy, c'est le samedi.»

«C'est vrai?» dit Marie-Laure.

«Eh oui,» dit Céline. «On est vendredi.»

«Ah bon,» dit Marie-Laure. «Quelle heure est-il?»

«Sept heures moins le quart,» dit Mathieu.

Et Marie-Laure dit: «Allons au café.»

Au café

Learning outcomes	Key language	Specific grammar and language awareness
• Names of snacks and drinks • Saying what you would like • Saying what you like and don't like • Understanding and saying prices in euros	• *Un café/ un sandwich au jambon, s'il vous plaît.* • *Deux/ trois euros cinquante…* • *C'est combien?*	• Understanding a 100 word text • Listening for detail • Use of definite article *le/ la* after *aimer* Flashcards 24 – 36

CD-ROM activities
1 Presentation of drinks and snacks
2 Decide if the drink or snack named matches the picture
3 Spot which of the passing trays goes with the order you hear
4 Identify the price of various snacks and drinks
5 Select the appropriate money for the prices you hear
6 Serve the ice cream flavours the customers ask for
7 Set the digital clock for the exact times named
8 Hunt round Petit Pont for someone who is eating or drinking a particular thing
+ Speaking activity

This unit introduces the words for various **drinks and snacks**, and recycles previous language including **numbers** – this time **in the form of prices**.

Page 23

Present the new vocabulary using flashcards 24 – 31 or Unit 5 Activity 1 on the CD-ROM. Take care to insist on an equal weighting of the syllables in words like *coca, café, sandwich, jambon* and *paquet,* emphasising how those which appear familiar have a different sound in French. Point out, if children do not notice it themselves, that the word *café* has two meanings in French: "café" and "coffee". Ask them to guess why this is. In the same way, the word 'tea' in English can refer to both a drink and a meal.

Use one or two flashcard games to practise these:

• Play a game where first you, then selected children, mime eating or drinking something, which the rest of the class has to guess from the actions.
• Play a cumulative game where eight volunteers line up in front of the class. The first child says: *Sur la table il y a un jus d'orange.* The second child repeats this, adding another item, and so on.

1 CD TRACK 29

Children listen to **four conversations at the café** and circle the things ordered by the customers.

Transcript:

Bonjour.

Bonjour. Un thé, s'il vous plaît.

Oui, madame.

Bonjour, monsieur.

Bonjour. Je voudrais un café, s'il vous plaît. Et un sandwich au fromage.

Oui, monsieur.

Bonjour.

Bonjour. Je voudrais un jus d'orange et un paquet de chips, s'il vous plaît.

Très bien.

Bonjour, mademoiselle.

Bonjour. Un sandwich au jambon et un coca, s'il vous plaît.

Merci.

Play a **memory game** where you stand four flashcards of people (Petit Pont 1, nos. 1 – 4) in a row at the front of the class. Now, one at a time, allocate some or all of the food and drink flashcards to the four people, asking children to name the items as you lay them on top of the 'people' cards. Next, turn the four sets of cards so they all have their backs to the class and ask a volunteer to name one of the characters and say what they are having, e.g. *Monsieur Moulin prend un café et un sandwich au jambon.* Check their statement by asking them to turn over the appropriate set of cards one after the other. The second time, allow children themselves to lay out the cards.

CD-ROM activities 2 and 3 offer further reinforcement of the topic.

Page **24**

1 Read together the speech bubbles on the café scene. In groups of three, taking turns to be the waiter, who has to repeat the order, **children can then improvise or rehearse variants** of the same conversation. These could be recorded or videoed.

2 Once again, encourage children to **express their own likes and dislikes** by asking each other about the same items of food and drink. Three types of answer are modelled in the book, of which the second encourages them to go one step further: *Oui, mais je préfère le jus d'orange.* Give a full example of each type of question and answer before expecting children to produce their own. Why not go one step further and introduce the phrases *C'est bon pour la santé* (It's good for you) and *C'est mauvais pour la santé* (It's not good for you)?

Introduce prices independently before linking them to the food and drink. Start with whole numbers, getting children first to repeat, then to produce the appropriate prices as you write them up or show them on cards. Insist on a good pronunciation of the word *euro(s)* itself, and draw attention to the fact that, as usual in French, the 's' of the plural is not heard. The inconsistency of the spoken and the written forms of prices, with the euro symbol after a written price (2,50 €) but the word *euros* in the middle of the spoken price (*deux euros cinquante*) can confuse some children and may require clarification, though the £ symbol is no more logical.

Children will get more out of the topic if they are given the opportunity to see and handle real euro currency. Take the time to talk about how much euros are worth in relation to pounds, and about which countries use them, being sure to start from what children themselves know.

If you have enough money available, they will enjoy handling it individually or in groups. Say a price (pick simpler ones to begin with) and ask children to select the right coins to make up that amount. They could then continue this in pairs, with one naming a price and the other finding the right money.

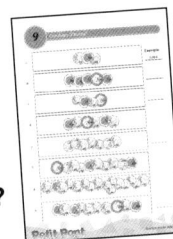

Copymaster 9
Combien d'euros?

The sheet comprises eight illustrations of **different combinations of euro coins**. Children have to work out and write down the value of each combination. More able children could be asked to write their answers in words.

Answers:

a 2,00 €

b 6,00 €

c 3,20 €

d 5,50 €

e 1, 45 €

f 3,50 €

g 2,50 €

h 5,00 €

3 Once children are confident enough with prices, look together at the **café price list** on page 24, asking children to say the prices. Ask questions in the form *C'est combien, un coca?* Children can then take turns asking each other similar questions, following the examples in the book.

Listening comprehension of prices, and further practice with money, are available in CD-ROM activities 4 and 5.

4 Children work out the **combined prices of the items illustrated**, writing them in figures. Check their answers by asking them to name the items, then give the price, e.g. *Un sandwich au jambon et un café, c'est 2,60 €.*

Answers:

a 4,30 €

b 5,60 €

c 9,50 €

Page **25**

The topic of **ice creams** can be introduced directly through the **transactional dialogue** given at the top of the page:

Une glace, s'il vous plaît.

Quel parfum?

Chocolat.

This exchange is the most natural and avoids the need to introduce the form *une glace à la fraise* or *une glace au chocolat.*

Ask children whether they can think of an English word related to the French *glace* ("glacier") and *parfum.* Teach the five ice cream flavours using **flashcards 33 – 37**.

Play briefly a game where you pin or stick up the five flashcards at the front of the class and two children try to be the first to point to the flavour you name.

5 Children **colour in the ice cream scoops** in the pictures according to the colours given. Note: these colours need to be correct before they do the listening activity that follows.

6 CD TRACK 30

Children listen to four of the *Petit Pont* characters **saying which flavours they want** and write the name of the correct person below each of the illustrations they have coloured. Play the conversation straight through the first time, then play it again pausing after each choice to give children time to think and write. Finally, play it again so they can check what they have written.

Answers:

Marie-Laure

Youssef

Mélanie

Benoît

Transcript:

Tu veux une glace, Youssef?

Oui, je veux bien.

Quel parfum?

Vanille et... menthe, s'il vous plaît.

Et toi, Benoît?

Euh... chocolat vanille, s'il vous plaît.

Mélanie?

Pour moi...citron fraise.

Et Marie-Laure?

Chocolat fraise, s'il vous plaît.

CD-ROM activity 6 offers interactive practice at recognising the different flavours.

🔘 **CD TRACK 31 Chanson**

This song follows the **same tune and cumulative pattern** as the original *Qu'est-ce qu'il y a à Petit Pont?* A **new item is added to each verse** and can be **cued by showing the appropriate flashcard**.

Transcript:

Qu'est-ce qu'on prend au Café du Pont?

Une glace à la fraise

Et un sandwich au jambon.

Qu'est-ce qu'on prend au Café du Pont?

Un jus d'orange

Une glace à la fraise

Et un sandwich au jambon.

Qu'est-ce qu'on prend au Café du Pont?

Un sandwich au fromage

Un jus d'orange

Une glace à la fraise

Et un sandwich au jambon.

Qu'est-ce qu'on prend au Café du Pont?

Une limonade

Un sandwich au fromage

Un jus d'orange

Une glace à la fraise

Et un sandwich au jambon.

Qu'est-ce qu'on prend au Café du Pont?

Un paquet de chips

Une limonade

Un sandwich au fromage

Un jus d'orange

Une glace à la fraise

Et un sandwich au jambon.

🔘 **CD TRACK 32 Poème**

A little verse that **rhymes the names of three of the places in town with three types of refreshment**. Play the recording first and ask children what they have understood. Then read through it together, explaining the new vocabulary *de l'eau* and *j'ai déjà pris*, before asking children to practise saying it aloud. Encourage them to emphasise the rhymes. They could then learn it for a homework.

Transcript:

Poème

Il fait chaud. Tu veux de l'eau?

Non merci. J'ai déjà pris

un thé au café,

une glace sur la place,

et une limonade au stade.

Moi, ça va!

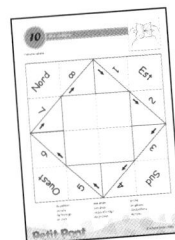

**Copymaster 10
Ma salière**

This sheet enables children to make a *salière* (everyone knows these 'snapdragon' type folded paper devices but what is the English for them?).

- They should begin by cutting out the main large square.

- The next stage is to write a word or phrase on the printed lines in each of the eight black-framed triangles. For this, they should choose the names of different food and drink items from the menu printed on the sheet. If possible, demonstrate this on an OHP, showing how this writing is to be read from the centre of the square. These words will be the 'results' that they will reveal by unfolding the appropriate segment when their partners have made their choices of compass points, then of numbers. (If you want to make the game more fun, replace some of the suggested food and drink words with things they dislike and will be more displeased to 'win', e.g. *épinards*, *escargots* or *cuisses de grenouille*).

- They are now ready to do the paper folding, which you should demonstrate clearly, step by step, from the front. If you are not an experienced *salière* maker, be sure to practise a few before you try to lead the activity!

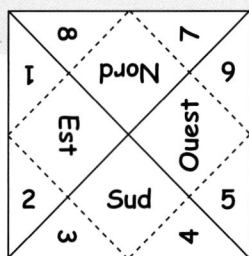

figure 1

For this, they will need to turn the sheet with the writing face down. They then fold in all four corners, to meet neatly in the middle (figure 1). Next, they turn the resulting smaller square over and do the same thing again, folding its corners to meet in the middle (figure 2). They can then put their thumbs and index fingers up under the flaps and play the game (figure 3).

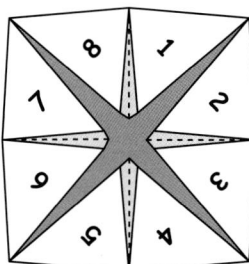

figure 2

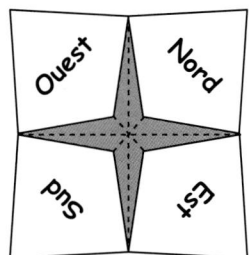

figure 3

- Their partner chooses a compass point, e.g. *ouest*, and the child recites *nord, sud, est, ouest* opening the 'beak' of the *salière* once for each word. The partner then chooses one of the numbers visible inside and the child counts up to that number, opening it each time. The partner then chooses one of the numbers that are showing and opens the corresponding flap to see which food or drink they have 'won'.

1 This **email** is the **longest text** children will have met **in the book so far**. It recycles words and structures from previous units but – apart from the guessable *montagnes* – includes no new vocabulary.

You can either read through it together or let children tackle it on their own or in pairs. The same applies to the questions that follow.

Answers:

a *To watch a (France v Ireland) football match on TV*

b *In February*

c *Cold but sunny*

d *Hot chocolate*

e *With his brother*

As a follow up activity, you could ask children to **find (orally or in writing**, individually or in groups) **the French for particular phrases in the email**:

this evening	*ce soir*
on television	*à la télé*
your favourite sport	*ton sport préféré*
to the Alps	*dans les Alpes*
in the morning	*le matin*
we go into a café	*on va dans un café*
in the afternoon	*l'après-midi*
it's great!	*c'est génial!*
where you live	*là où tu habites*
here's a photo	*voici une photo*

This activity is also available as a **matching exercise on copymaster 12** and provides good reinforcement if this has first been done orally.

**Copymaster 11
Email**

Reading and writing follow up to the email on page 26.

1 Children have to find the English for ten phrases from the email and connect them by lines to the French.

Answers: see above.

2 A **crossword**, based on the email.

Solution:

A	V	E	C		R	È	G	L	E
L			H		E				
P	A	P	A		G	O	M	M	E
E			U		A			O	N
S		A	D	O	R	E		N	
	T			D		E	T		
F	É	V	R	I	E	R		A	
	L			R	O	U	G	E	
M	É	T	É	O		S		N	
	U			D	E		E	T	

3 Children are asked to write their own answers to the three questions in the email.

Page **27** CD TRACK 33 Pronunciation

Let children **identify the sound common to these words** (-*eur*) for themselves. Practise saying them together, **emphasising the length of the syllable**. Take the opportunity to see whether they remember the meaning of the words too.

> **Transcript:**
>
> *euro, couleur, heure, professeur, soeur, visiteur, facteur.*

Contre la montre

A chance for children to see how quickly they can read off the list of prices. Encourage them to time each other. It is up to you whether you put the emphasis on their trying to improve their own performance or whether you make the activity competitive.

CD TRACK 34 **Story: Domino a faim**

As usual, children can either listen to you telling the story, using the text below, or they can listen to the recorded version of it. You could follow this by **drawing up a list of the places Domino goes to**, the people he meets and the food he is offered. On a second or subsequent telling, pause to let children supply some or all of this information as it arises, e.g. *Domino va à la...[place]...... Youssef et.... [Mathieu] sont sur la place. Ils mangent des.....[chips].*

Like the other stories, this one can be acted out once children have become familiar with it.

Make sure you point out the spelling of the expression *miam! miam!* which nevertheless sounds exactly like a British Southerner's pronunciation of "yum! yum!" when repeated a number of times.

Transcript:

Domino a faim

C'est le mercredi trois février. Il est neuf heures du matin. A Petit Pont il fait beau mais il fait froid. Domino a faim.

«Pauvre Domino!» dit Céline. «Il n'y a rien à manger!»

«C'est bon,» dit maman. «On va aller au centre commercial.»

«Non, pas toi, Domino,» dit Céline. «Tu gardes la maison.»

Alors, à neuf heures et demie, maman et Céline partent au centre commercial. Mais Domino n'est pas content. Il a faim.

Domino va à la place. Youssef et Mathieu sont sur la place. Ils mangent des chips.

«Bonjour, Domino,» dit Mathieu. «Tu veux des chips?»

Et Mathieu donne des chips à Domino. Youssef aussi.

«Miam! Miam!» dit Domino. Et il part.

Sur le pont il y a Benoît. Benoît mange un gâteau.

«Tu veux du gâteau?» dit Benoît.

Et Benoît donne un morceau de gâteau à Domino.

«Miam! Miam!» dit Domino. Et il part.

Devant le café un monsieur mange un sandwich au jambon.

«Bonjour, chien,» dit le monsieur. «Tu veux un morceau?»

Et le monsieur donne un morceau de sandwich à Domino.

«Miam! Miam!» dit Domino. Et il part.

Mélanie est devant sa maison. Elle mange du chocolat.

«Tu veux un morceau?» dit Mélanie.

Et elle donne un morceau de chocolat à Domino.

«Miam! Miam!» dit Domino. Et il part. Il est content. Il a mangé: des chips, du gâteau, du sandwich et du chocolat.

Il est midi. Domino rentre à la maison. Céline et sa maman arrivent du centre commercial. «Brrrr! Il fait froid,» dit Céline. «Pauvre Domino! Tu as faim, non? Voici ton déjeuner.»

Et elle donne un bol de croquettes à Domino.

Domino ne dit rien.

Unité 6 — Les vêtements

Learning outcomes
- Items of clothing
- Saying what you or someone else are wearing
- Saying what colour someone's clothes are
- Giving your opinion about different clothes
- Describing details of a picture

Key language
- Je/ qui/ il/ elle porte…
- un t-shirt jaune/ une robe bleue

Specific grammar and language awareness
- Word order of nouns and adjectives
- Agreement of colour adjectives
- *mon, ma, mes* (recognition only)

Flashcards 37 – 47

CD-ROM activities
1 Presentation of articles of clothing
2 Click on the named items of clothing to stop them blowing off the line
3 Use the torch beam to find the articles of clothing described (including colour)
4 Listen to the descriptions in order to colour the children's clothing correctly
5 Select the appropriate words from a 'menu' to describe the pictures
6 Listen to statements and attach the correct price tag to each item of clothing
7 Type in the missing letters in gapped names of clothes
8 Watch an animated sequence, then answer questions about it
+ Speaking activity

Introduce the clothes vocabulary using flashcards 37 – 46 and/or activity 1 on the CD-ROM, paying attention to the use of the correct determinant *un*, *une* or *des*. Note the pronunciation of the word sweat, which the French pronounce like the English "sweet". Play two or three flashcard games and a drawing game where you or a child starts a drawing and the others have to guess as soon as possible what it is.

CD-ROM activity 2 offers a fun way of reinforcing this vocabulary.

Borrowings from English

You may like to take this opportunity to talk about what happens when words are borrowed from one language to another: the French *jean, baskets* and *pull* have all undergone changes in the process (in this case mainly abbreviation). Ask them where they think the word *basket* may have come from (what you wear when playing basketball). If children find this amusing, remind them that English has distorted expressions borrowed from French too, e.g. there is no such thing as an "*en suite*" in France, and the abbreviation RSVP used on invitations, supposedly meaning *Répondez, s'il vous plaît*, simply doesn't exist in French. This may be a good moment at which to ask children who know other languages whether they know any words which have been absorbed into English. The names for types of food are probably the most common.

Next, **introduce the verb *porte***, saying what you yourself are wearing, using only the known vocabulary, e.g. *Je porte une jupe, un sweat et des chaussures*. Ask children what they think *Je porte* means. Then ask them to tell their partner what *they* are wearing. Finally, encourage them to help you describe what other people are wearing, using the same verb, e.g.: *Benjamin porte une chemise, un pantalon et des chaussures*.

Page 28

1 You can now look at the picture in the book and ask children to say what the characters are wearing. Having done that, they can do the first activity, writing in who is wearing each of the things named.

Answers:

un pull: le professeur

une robe: Mme Duval

une jupe: Mélanie

un t-shirt: Mathieu

un jean: Mathieu

un pantalon: le professeur

des chaussures: le professeur et Mme Duval

des baskets: Mathieu

un sweat: Mélanie

une chemise: le professeur

2 This pairwork involves one child making an assertion about what one of the characters is wearing, and their partner looking at the picture and deciding whether it is true or false. They should take turns to make up the sentences. Be sure to model several examples before asking children to do it on their own.

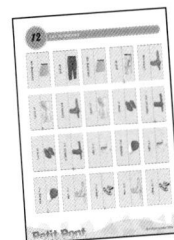

Copymaster 12
Les dominoes

Nothing to do with the dog, this is a game for children to play in pairs. Each card has a word for an item of clothing in one half and the picture of another item of clothing in the other. Cut up the domino cards and show them how to deal five each and put the rest face down in a pile. Children then take turns to lay a domino, saying the French for the word and picture they are matching. They should pick up another card from the pile if they can't go. The first to get rid of their dominos is the winner.

Page 29

3 Children have already said what they are wearing, but now they are asked to write it down. This only requires them to select and copy the appropriate words from the opposite page.

CD TRACK 35

An additional listening to give more **practice at recognising the words for clothes**.

They are asked to look back at the pictures on page 1 of the book, then listen to the statements and decide whether they are true or false. They can either show their opinion directly or write down *v(rai)* or *f(aux)* to be checked afterwards. In either case, encourage them to correct those that are wrong.

Answers:

Mathieu porte un t-shirt jaune. Il porte un jean bleu.

Mélanie porte une jupe rouge et un sweat gris.

Le professeur porte une chemise blanche, un pull vert et un pantalon marron.

CD-ROM activity 3 presents further examples of colour adjectives with clothing.

CD TRACK 36 Song

The song is based on the **comical situation of Youssef coming out of the swimming pool and finding that his clothes are missing**. As they join in, children should **mime the actions** of him putting on the clothes in the first verse, taking them off in the second, and panicking in the third!

Ensure that they understand the **expressions of weather and time** that appear in the verses. *Vieux* is new vocabulary. Challenge children to be the first to guess the meaning of the **new verbs *je mets*, *j'enlève*, and *je sors*** from the miming of the actions. This is the first time they have seen the **possessive adjectives *mon*, *ma* and *mes***. However, the parallel with *ton*, *ta* and *tes* introduced with parts of the body, together with the context – not to mention their similarity to the English "my" – , should make them confident to guess at their meaning.

Before **linking the colour words to clothes**, you may want to do some **quick revision of the colours** themselves. At its most basic level this can be done using flashcards 32 to 42. But make sure you use them in sentences as well, holding up a felt tip, for example, and asking *Le feutre est bleu, blanc ou rouge?* or *La trousse est blanche, grise ou verte?*

4 You can differentiate the next step by either moving straight on to activity 4 or by asking some questions first about the colours of the clothes worn by the people in the picture. Children will have seen examples of colour adjectives coming after the noun in Petit Pont 1, Unit 7, but may need to be reminded of this. This is best done by giving three children a piece of paper with a word on it: *un/ t-shirt/ bleu*, then *une jupe/ rouge*, and asking them to physically hold them up in the right order at the front of the class.

They can then **circle the right colour adjectives** in the sentences describing the picture.

Transcript:

Il fait beau aujourd'hui.
Je vais à la piscine.

Je mets mon vieux jean.
Je mets mes baskets.
Je mets mon T-shirt.
Je mets ma casquette.

A deux heures et demie
J'arrive à la piscine.

J'enlève mon vieux jean.
J'enlève mes baskets.
J'enlève mon T-shirt.
J'enlève ma casquette.

A cinq heures et demie
Je sors de la piscine.

Où est mon vieux jean?!
Où sont mes baskets?!
Où est mon T-shirt?!
Où est ma casquette?!

The activities on this double page are designed to **reinforce the language of clothing and colours**, both in terms of vocabulary and structures, introduced so far. Activity 4 recycles expressions of weather, left and right, and telling the time as well.

1 These jumbled words focus children's minds on the **spelling of the items of clothing**.

> Answers:
>
> **a** *jupe*
>
> **b** *pantalon*
>
> **c** *baskets*
>
> **d** *chemise*
>
> **e** *casquette*

2 This item gives children the opportunity to demonstrate their understanding of two fundamental differences between French and English: the **order of noun and adjective**, and the fact that the **verb in the present tense is always just one word in French**. The colour coding in the sentences to be compared will help them with the grammatical terms used.

Copymaster 13
Qui porte quoi?

1 Ten questions about **who is wearing what** in the story illustrations on page 27 of the pupils' book.

> Answers:
>
> *Qui porte une chemise verte? Mme Duval*
>
> *Qui porte un sweat rouge? Benoît*
>
> *Qui porte une chemise violette? Youssef*
>
> *Qui porte un t-shirt rose? Céline*
>
> *Qui porte un jean bleu? Youssef et Benoît*
>
> *Qui porte un short bleu? Mathieu*
>
> *Qui porte des chaussures jaunes? Mme Duval*
>
> *Qui porte une chemise blanche? Le monsieur (au café)*
>
> *Qui porte une jupe bleue? Mme Duval*
>
> *Qui porte un t-shirt blanc, vert et rose? Mélanie*

2 Children have to **colour the picture** according to the instructions.

An interactive version of this, but with audio instructions rather than written instructions, is available in CD-ROM activity 4.

Contre la montre

Children have to see how quickly they can **describe the clothes on the washing line**. Depending on the class, you can either prepare the French together or leave them to work it out for themselves. If they time themselves, you could then ask *Alors, combien de secondes?*, insisting that they give their answer in French.

> Answers:
>
> *Il y a un t-shirt blanc, un jean bleu, une chemise verte, une robe marron, une casquette jaune, une jupe rouge, un t-shirt rose et un pantalon noir.*

CD-ROM activity 5 provides further practice of word order with colour adjectives.

3 This word sequencing task highlights the **position of the colour adjectives** in the French sentences.

Answers:

a *Amélie porte un t-shirt rose.*

b *Je porte une chemise bleue.*

c *Benoît porte un sweat rouge.*

Children could be invited to challenge each other by writing and then muddling up similar sentences of their own.

4 This game of '**spot the difference**' is best played individually or in pairs, then checked as a plenary with the whole class, possibly in writing as well as orally. All children will be able to identify differences; differentiation will occur in their ability to put these into words. Encourage them as far as possible to formulate a phrase or sentence in French to describe each difference they discover. Do this by inviting someone to spot a first difference and helping them to put it into words. For example, a child may say: *les sandwichs.* Ask: *Il y a combien de sandwichs?* They may answer: *deux sandwichs et trois sandwichs.* Develop this by saying: *Oui. Dans 'a' il y a deux sandwichs et dans 'b' il y a trois sandwichs.* Some children may be able to write down in French the differences they find.

If you have a **dressing up box** in school, this can provide the opportunity for an enjoyable practical game. Ask one or two volunteers: *Est-ce qu'il y a un pantalon gris?/ une jupe rose?* etc, which they have to find and hold up. If appropriate, you could ask them to put on the named item: *Mets un chapeau noir.*

CD-ROM activities 6, 7 and 8 offer further reinforcement of clothes vocabulary, as well as revision of language from previous units.

1 This **speaking pairwork** requires some pictures from a magazine or catalogue, which children could be asked to bring in. The idea is for them to give their **opinions on various clothes** using the expressions for **likes and dislikes** that they already know, and naming the items of clothing where possible. To start them off, take a few pictures and ask individuals *Tu aimes ça?/ Tu aimes le pantalon?*

This could be developed into a display, in which they cut out pictures and create captions along the lines of the dialogue in the book: *Tu aimes les baskets? Cool, la jupe!*

Answers:

a	b
Il est deux heures et demie.	*Il est deux heures et quart.*
Il fait beau.	*Il fait gris.*
Domino est à gauche.	*Domino est à droite.*
Le t-shirt de Marie-Laure est jaune.	*Le t-shirt de Marie-Laure est bleu.*
Les baskets de Benoît sont blancs.	*Les baskets de Benoît sont noirs.*
Il y a deux sandwichs.	*Il y a trois sandwichs.*
Mathieu porte une chemise blanche.	*Mathieu porte un t-shirt blanc.*
La casquette de Youssef est rouge.	*La casquette de Youssef est verte.*
Céline mange une glace blanche.	*Céline mange une glace rouge.*
Benoît a/ boit un coca.	*Benoît a/ boit un jus d'orange.*

CD TRACK 37 **Pronunciation**

Before practising the pronunciation by repetition at different volumes and in different tones, encourage children to identify for themselves the *–ère* sound common to these words. They can then be asked to work out how many different ways there are of spelling it (*er, aire, ère*). Ensure that they know the meaning of all the words.

> **Transcript:**
>
> *vert, père, mercredi, mère, super, frère, anniversaire, rivière, documentaire.*

CD TRACK 38 **Story**

Before reading the story or letting children hear the recording, say a few words about *carnaval*. *Carnaval* is a significant event in the year for all French children. It is celebrated in primary schools by children dressing up and often parading in the street. This is a good opportunity to introduce the key word *déguisé* (dressed up) before you begin.

Many of the new words are cognate and can be easily guessed with the help of a little mime if necessary: *pirate, princesse, excité, clown* (pronounced "cloon"), *tigre, masque, cap, gobelin, robot, monstre, téléphone, panique.* Remember to pronounce Harry Potter in the French way with equal stress on each of the syllables: "Arípoter". If children do not immediately recognise the name, write it up as you repeat it – a perfect demonstration of the difference that stress can make!

As usual, children can look at the pictures in the book or on the interactive whiteboard to help their understanding while they listen to the story.

> **Transcript:**
>
> Carnaval
>
> *En février c'est carnaval à Petit Pont. Le jour de carnaval, tous les enfants se déguisent.*
>
> *A la maison, Mathieu se déguise en pirate. Sa soeur Amélie se déguise en princesse, mais – elle n'est pas contente.*
>
> – *Je ne veux pas être princesse, dit Amélie. C'est stupide!*
>
> – *Mais elle est jolie, ta robe, dit Mme Bertrand.*
>
> – *Je n'aime pas la robe! dit Amélie.*
>
> – *Mais c'est une belle couleur, dit Mme Bertrand.*
>
> – *Je n'aime pas la couleur! dit Amélie.*
>
> *A neuf heures, les enfants arrivent à l'école. Tout le monde est très excité.*
>
> *Youssef est déguisé en clown.*
>
> *Sa soeur Farida est déguisée en sorcière. Elle porte une longue jupe verte, un t-shirt vert, et un chapeau vert pointu.*
>
> *Nicolas est déguisé en Harry Potter.*
>
> *Mélanie est déguisée en tigre.*
>
> *Benoît est déguisé en Batman. Il porte une cape noire et un masque.*
>
> *Les petits sont déguisés en animaux, en gobelins, en robots, en monstres!*
>
> *Amélie n'est pas contente. Elle n'aime pas être princesse.*
>
> *A deux heures de l'après-midi, tous les élèves sortent de l'école. Ils traversent le pont et ils vont à la place de Petit Pont. Là, ils chantent et ils dansent. Après, ils rentrent à l'école. Ils boivent de la limonade et ils mangent du gâteau.*
>
> *A quatre heures et demie Mme Bertrand arrive à l'école pour chercher Amélie. Elle regarde dans la cour. Il y a un clown, un monstre et une sorcière, mais Amélie, la petite princesse, n'est pas là.*

– *Oh là là! dit Mme Bertrand. Où est Amélie?*

Elle va dans la salle de classe. Mais Amélie n'est pas là.

Elle traverse le pont et elle va sur la place. Mais Amélie n'est pas là.

Puis elle va à la maison. Amélie n'est pas là non plus.

Mme Bertrand téléphone à l'école.

– *Allô, dit-elle. C'est Mme Bertrand. Est-ce qu'Amélie est là?*

– *Non, dit le professeur. Elle n'est pas là.*

Mme Bertrand panique.

Puis, à ce moment, une petite sorcière arrive à la maison.

– *Mais... je ne comprends pas, dit Mme Bertrand.*

Amélie enlève son chapeau vert.

– *Je ne voulais pas être princesse. J'ai échangé avec Farida. Farida est princesse maintenant. Et moi, je suis sorcière!*

A la maison

<table>
<tr><td>Learning outcomes</td><td>Key language</td></tr>
<tr><td>● Rooms in the house</td><td>● Où est…? Where is…?
● Il est/ elle est dans le/ la… It's/ He's/ She's in the….</td></tr>
</table>

Page 33

Ask children to look at the picture of **Céline's house** on page 33, with the rooms and garden labelled. Say the names aloud and ask them to find and point to the labels as they hear them. Then ask the class to repeat them after you, saying each one as many times as is necessary and breaking them down into parts to ensure correct pronunciation. Insist on the correct definite article, *le* or *la*, too.

Page 34

1 By looking at the picture, children have to **say where each of the people is**. This should be done orally first, then they can write the answers in the spaces provided with as much or as little support as you see fit.

Answers:

Où est Céline?	Dans la cuisine.
Où est Charlotte?	Dans la chambre.
Où est Mathieu?	Dans le salon.
Où est Madame Thomas?	Dans la salle de bains.
Où est Monsieur Thomas?	Dans la salle à manger
Où est Domino?	Dans le jardin.

2 In this activity children again have to **look for things** in the picture and **say where they are**, but this time they have to link the written descriptions of the things with the written names of the rooms. Differentiate by the amount of preparation you offer, e.g. getting children to read the lists aloud or talking through the whole matching process with them. Insist that they draw in the lines "*en crayon*". Mark the answers by asking volunteers to read out the phrases that go together.

Answers:

la casquette rouge — dans le salon

la jupe bleue — dans la salle à manger

la table marron — dans la cuisine

la télévision — dans la salle de bains

le drapeau français — dans la chambre

3 CD TRACK 39

Children can now **listen to a series of conversations** in which people are asking where other things (not shown in the main house picture) are. First play the recording and ask what they think the conversations are about. Next, ask them to look at the drawings in the book, eliciting the names of each thing or room illustrated. Then play the conversations again, one at a time. Children now draw lines to link each illustrated object to the appropriate room. Depending on the class, these can either be checked one at a time or after they have completed all five.

Transcript:

1

Céline: *Maman, où est mon livre de français?*

Maman: *Ton livre de français? Il est dans la salle à manger.*

2

Papa: *Oh là là! Où il est, mon sandwich?*

Céline: *Oh papa. Il est dans la cuisine.*

Papa: *Ah bon?*

3

Charlotte: *Où sont mes baskets?*

Maman: *Elles sont dans la salle de bains.*

Charlotte: *Ah, merci.*

4

Céline: *Je ne trouve pas mon jean.*

Charlotte: *Ton jean? Il est dans ta chambre, non?*

Céline: *Mais non. Ah si! Le voilà.*

5

Charlotte: *C'est pas possible! Où sont mes bonbons?*

Maman: *Je ne sais pas, moi.*

Charlotte: *Céline, tu as vu mes bonbons?*

Céline: *Non.*

Charlotte: *Papa, tu as vu mes bonbons?*

Papa: *Je crois qu'ils sont dans le salon.*

Charlotte: *Ah oui, c'est vrai! Qui veut un bonbon?*

Answers:

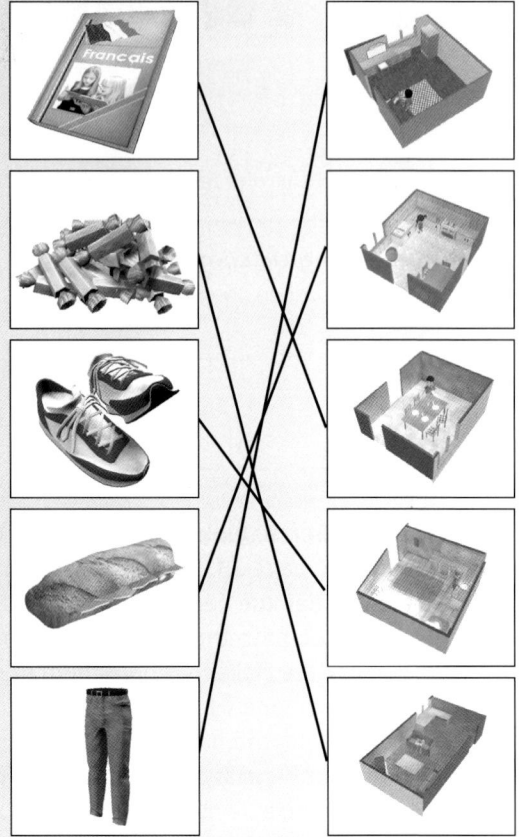

4 Children can now try to **invent a similar conversation** themselves in pairs or groups, in which one of them is asking where something is. Be sure to model a sample conversation first, based on one of the recordings.

5 Finally, children can **make their own version of one (or more) of the signs** in the book, **to put up on their bedroom door** at home. Read them together and encourage them to guess at or look up their meaning.

Ma journée

Learning outcomes	Key language	Specific grammar and language awareness
• Daily routine: saying what time you get up, go to school, etc. • Weekday and weekend activities • School subjects • Saying which subjects you like and dislike • Asking for what you want at a baker's • The main types of shop	• Je me lève/ je vais à l'école/ je mange/ je rentre/ je vais au lit • à/ vers sept heures • -er verbs: je regarde/ mange/ joue/ rentre/ j'aime • je voudrais	• Use of definite article le/ la after aimer • é and è Flashcards 48 – 70

CD-ROM activities

1 Presentation of five aspects of daily routine
2 Select the visual that goes with the sentence you hear
3 Match the names of school subjects to the symbols
4 Select the school subject and facial expression to match the opinion you hear
5 Select what each customer asks for in the baker's shop, and put it on the counter
6 Select the correct words to fill the gaps in sentences describing four short animations
7 Identify the word that rhymes, and burst the bubble
8 Look around Petit Pont for someone who fits the description, following the advice given by characters you meet
+ Speaking activity

Using flashcards 48 and 52, together with appropriate actions, introduce the expressions *Je me lève* and *Je vais au lit*, getting children first to repeat them with you, then to produce them themselves as you show the pictures. (There is no need to refer explicitly to the fact that *je me lève* is a reflexive verb. They learned several persons of the verb *s'appeler* early on without this ever becoming an issue and can add this new example to their vocabulary in the same way. If any children make the connection, so much the better.) Next,

stand or stick up the two flashcards with enough room between them for the three others that you will introduce (49 -51): *Je vais à l'école, Je mange à la cantine* and *Je rentre à la maison*. These three expressions with *à* may prompt a reminder that *à* can mean either "to" or "at". Place these flashcards in sequence between the first two, then, referring to all five, introduce the unit title: *Ma journée*, ensuring they understand that it means "my day". Help them make the connection with the word *jour*.

Play a number of flashcard and miming games to help children become familiar with the new language. Activities 1 and 2 on the CD-ROM can also be used here. You may want to introduce the written form at this stage, on page 35 of the book.

> ### False friends
>
> At this point you may like to talk about *faux amis* – words like *journée* and "journey" that look similar but in fact mean different things. Other examples are *voyage* (meaning "journey" in French), *pub* (short for *publicité*), *car* (meaning "coach") and *pain*. In German the words *Gift* meaning "poison" and *Mist* meaning "manure" are particularly good examples!

Next, **re-use the five expressions taught**, adding a time on the hour to each one, e.g. *Je me lève à huit heures. Je vais à l'école à neuf heures,* and so on. You could illustrate the times using a clock, or ask different children both to adjust the clock and to select the appropriate flashcard to match what you say. As you proceed, introduce times between the hours little by little. They should then be ready to tackle activity 1 in the book.

1 CD TRACK 40

Children listen to Jean-Philippe describing his day and have to circle the time he gives for each episode. Note that the common abbreviation '*h*' for *heures* is used in this activity. Rather than point this out yourself, ask children whether they have noticed anything about the way the times are written.

> **Transcript:**
>
> *Je me lève à sept heures et demie.*
>
> *A huit heures quinze, je vais à l'école.*
>
> *Je mange à la cantine à midi.*
>
> *A quatre heures et demie je rentre à la maison.*
>
> *Je vais au lit à dix heures.*

> **Answers:**
>
> *7h30, 8h15, 12h00, 4h30, 10h00.*

2 Children fill in the **real times** at which they do the same five things. They can either do this in figures, using the '*h*' form they have just met, or write them out in words. They should all use the expression *Je mange à la cantine,* even though bringing sandwiches is not an option in French state schools (they either eat the school meal or go home). When they have completed this, ask them to practise saying their sentences, including the times in French. They can then read these to their partners. Finally, hold up a flashcard and name a child, who has to say at what time they do the corresponding thing.

CD TRACK 41 Song

This song is about Benoît's mother getting more and more exasperated as she tries to get him up. Children can increase the urgency with each verse. The only new expression is *Tu es en retard.*

> **Transcript:**
>
> *Lève-toi vite! Lève-toi vite!*
> *Tu es en retard!*
> *Lève-toi vite! Lève-toi vite!*
> *Il est huit heures et quart!*
>
> *Lève-toi vite! Lève-toi vite!*
> *Il fait beau aujourd'hui!*
> *Lève-toi vite! Lève-toi vite!*
> *Il est huit heures et demie!*
>
> *Lève-toi vite! Lève-toi vite!*
> *Écoute-moi, Benoît!*
> *Lève-toi vite! Lève-toi vite!*
> *Il est neuf heures déjà!*
>
> *Lève-toi vite! Lève-toi vite!*
> *Tu as un visiteur!*
> *Lève-toi vite! Lève-toi vite!*
> *C'est ton professeur!*

Most of the names for **school subjects** look similar to their English equivalents. For this reason many children will find it helpful to see their written forms straight away. Flashcards 53–61can then be used to practise the pronunciation in one or two quick fire games. Whilst avoiding a general tendency to say them in an English way, pay particular attention to the pronunciation of *histoire, sciences* and *art*.

CD-ROM activity 3 offers another way of reinforcing this vocabulary.

🔘 **CD TRACK 42**

Follow up by asking the class to listen to the series of extracts from **real French lessons** and identify which subject it is. Ask them: *C'est quelle matière?*

This activity gives practice at what is **an essential strategy in foreign language learning**, namely **listening for key words and phrases** in the same way a climber feels for hand and footholds. In some extracts sound effects provide additional clues. It is worth emphasising to children that they should not expect and do not need to be able to understand everything in order to do the task successfully.

> **Transcript:**
>
> 1 *C'est parti. Un, deux…*
>
>   *La canne de Jeanne…*
>
> 2 *Pierre achète quatre gâteaux. Il paie en tout huit euros. Quelle est le prix d'un gâteau? Nous allons demander à Oscar.*
>
> 3 *En 1642 les soldats attaquent le château de Petit Pont. Les troupes du duc Ferdinand défendent le château. Il y a une grande bataille.*
>
> 4 *What time do you get up?*
>
>   *Eight o'clock.*
>
>   *What time do you get up, please, Philipinne?*
>
>   *Seven thirty.*
>
> 5 *Nous allons parler aujourd'hui des grandes chaînes de montagnes françaises. Dans le sud à la frontière avec l'Espagne, il y a… ?*
>
>   *Les Pyrénées.*
>
>   *Très bien. Alors, quelle chaîne de montagnes – très hautes montagnes – euh… se trouve placée à l'est de la France, avec… à la frontière plutôt avec l'Italie?*
>
>   *Les Alpes.*
>
>   *Excellent!*
>
> 6 *Allez, Mathieu! Passe le ballon! Allez, OK, oui – oui oui – non là – oui!*

Answers:

1 *musique*

2 *maths*

3 *histoire*

4 *anglais*

5 *géographie*

6 *sport*

1 Move on as soon as possible to the question about likes and dislikes, asking a few children yourself about different subjects to begin with, then using one pair to model a question and answer before allowing everyone to ask and answer the questions in pairs.

Then, rather than teaching the word *matières*, ask them to guess the meaning of the question *Quelle est ta matière préférée?* at the bottom of the page. Ensure that they can all ask as well as answer that question.

Page **37**

2 **CD TRACK 43**

Children listen to four of the Petit Pont characters saying what they think about **four school subjects** and fill in the mouths (smiley, or not smiley) on the chart accordingly. Before playing the recording, ask which subjects are illustrated on the chart. Allow them to hear each interview at least twice.

> **Transcript:**
>
> *Céline, tu aimes les maths?*
>
> *Oui, j'aime bien.*
>
> *Et les sciences?*
>
> *Oui, j'aime beaucoup.*
>
> *Tu aimes le sport?*
>
> *Ça va.*
>
> *Et la musique?*
>
> *Non, je n'aime pas ça.*

Benoît. Tu aimes les maths, toi?

Non, je déteste les maths.

Tu aimes les sciences?

Oui, ça va.

Et le sport?

Oui, j'adore ça.

Tu aimes la musique aussi?

Oui, j'aime bien.

Marie-Laure, tu aimes les maths, toi?

Les maths, ça va.

Et les sciences?

Oui, j'aime ça.

Tu aimes le sport?

Non, je n'aime pas beaucoup.

Et la musique?

Oui, c'est ma matière préférée.

Mathieu, tu aimes les maths?

Oui, j'aime bien.

Tu aimes les sciences?

Oui.

Et le sport?

Ça va.

Tu aimes la musique?

Je déteste la musique.

C'est vrai?

Ah oui. Je n'aime pas ça.

Answers:

Prénom	Maths	Sciences	Sport	Musique
Céline	☺	☺	☺	☹
Benoît	☹	☺	☺	☺
Marie-Laure	☺	☺	☹	☺
Mathieu	☺	☺	☺	☹

For more practice, see CD-ROM activity 4.

64

CD TRACK 44 Poème

As well as reinforcing the names of the school subjects, this verse reintroduces the expression *c'est pas mal,* first introduced in Petit Pont 1. Children may like to create their own version of it by reorganising the combinations of subject and comment, and introducing, if they want to, the verb *je déteste.*

Transcript:

Les maths, c'est pas mal.

J'aime bien la musique.

L'histoire, ça va.

Et l'art plastique.

Les sciences, c'est pas mal.

J'aime bien le français.

La géo, ça va.

J'aime bien l'anglais.

Mais le sport,

Ça, j'adore!

CD TRACK 45 Et le week-end, qu'est-ce que tu fais?

A series of six sentences in which **Mathieu summarises what he does at weekends**. Listen to and/ or read through the sentences, inviting children to put them into English and guess at the meaning of the new vocabulary *vers, jeu-vidéo* and *copains.* You may want to practise a few examples of the time using *vers* (meaning "at about") rather than *à.*

Transcript:

Et le week-end, qu'est-ce que tu fais?

Je me lève vers neuf heures et demie.

Le matin je regarde la télé ou je joue à un jeu-vidéo.

L'après-midi je joue avec mes copains.

Je vais au centre commercial ou à la piscine.

Le soir on mange vers huit heures.

Je vais au lit vers dix heures.

3 Children should now put together **a statement** of their own **about what they do at weekends**. These will inevitably vary in length, as well as in the extent to which they are based on Mathieu's answer; some children may use writing to prepare a fundamentally oral statement whilst others can be helped to produce an accurate written version too. Versions of the model sentences, with the variables highlighted in colour or replaced by gaps, can be provided to support this activity.

Copymaster 14
Le tour de Petit Pont

This sheet provides a **reading activity in the guise of a board game**, to be played with a die and two place markers. It includes a range of verbs and verb phrases such as *Tu as faim, tu regardes, tu cherches, tu joues, tu veux jouer, tu as perdu, tu as oublié,* as well as reinforcing the vocabulary of places in town.

Page **38**

CD TRACK 46 A la boulangerie

This item **recycles the language used for ordering things in a café** and for prices in the context of the baker's. Children will have met the word *boulangerie* before and may have seen the sign for it when moving round Petit Pont on the CD-ROM.

Begin by going over the **numbers 60, 70, 80 and 90** at the top of the page. These of course are like little sums themselves when translated literally and children can be encouraged to explain *why* they mean what they mean. Next introduce the names for the four bakery items using flashcards 62 – 65 and playing one or two games with these. (The ideal, of course, would be to bring in a few real ones for children to sample!) Then look together at the price list in red and ask a few questions about it, e.g. *C'est combien, un pain aux raisins/ une baguette?* Children can now listen to the dialogue. Read through it next phrase by phrase, with everyone repeating it after you. Ask them what they think *je voudrais* means. They can then work in pairs, first acting out the dialogue as it is, then amending it by changing the elements printed in red. These variations could be performed in front of the class or recorded. **Flashcards 62 – 65** could be printed several times and cut out to provide 'props', and real euros used if possible.

Transcript:

– *Bonjour.*

– *Bonjour. Je voudrais deux baguettes et deux pains au chocolat, s'il vous plaît.*

– *Voilà. Ça fait deux euros quatre-vingts.*

– *Merci.*

– *Merci. Au revoir.*

1 CD TRACK 47

Five dialogues set at the baker's. Children should listen to each one at least twice and write down – individually or in pairs – what the people are buying. On a subsequent listening they can try to identify the total price, which could be verified by doing the calculation together. See whether they spot the expression *Bonne journée* in three of the dialogues, pointing them back to the unit title if they do not guess straight away what it means.

Transcript:

1

– *Bonjour, madame.*

– *Bonjour. Je voudrais une baguette, s'il vous plaît.*

– *Voilà. Quatre-vingts centimes.*

– *Merci.*

– *Merci. Au revoir.*

2

– *Bonjour.*

– *Bonjour. Je voudrais trois pains au chocolat, s'il vous plaît.*

– *Voilà. Ça fait un euro quatre-vingts.*

– *Merci.*

– *Merci. Bonne journée.*

3

– *Bonjour.*

– *Bonjour. Je voudrais deux croissants et deux baguettes, s'il vous plaît.*

– *Voilà. Ça fait deux euros soixante.*

– *Merci.*

– *Merci. Au revoir.*

4

– *Bonjour, monsieur.*

– *Bonjour. Je voudrais un pain aux raisins et un pain au chocolat, s'il vous plaît.*

– *Un euro quarante, s'il vous plaît.*

– *Merci.*

– *Merci. Bonne journée.*

5

– *Bonjour.*

– *Bonjour. Je voudrais trois baguettes et deux pains au raisins, s'il vous plaît.*

– *Voilà. Ça fait quatre euros.*

– *Merci.*

– *Merci. Bonne journée.*

For further interactive practice of this language, see CD-ROM activity 5.

Having been to the bakers, children can now learn the **names of four other types of shop**: *l'épicerie, la boucherie, la pharmacie* and *le supermarché*. Present these, together with *la boulangerie*, using **flashcards 66 – 70** and/ or the pictures on page 36. Children should be able to see the similarity of *boucherie* and *supermarché* to the English, and may be familiar with the word "pharmacy" too. Point out that the word *épicerie* comes from *épices* meaning "spice", and is now generally used to refer to any small food store.

The danger – or temptation, if you prefer – of shops and shopping as a topic is that it brings with it a potential avalanche of new vocabulary. Here, a minimum of new words is introduced, just enough to be able to relate two names of product to each new type of shop. If you (or the children) want to add to this vocabulary base, it is up to you.

2 This activity requires children to **link up the shops to the appropriate products** using pencil lines. The products illustrated are labelled and some should be known already, but the pictures are enough for children to be able to complete the task. You can then reinforce the French names when checking their answers.

Supermarché is not included since you can buy just about anything there – though note that French supermarkets are not allowed by law to sell medicinal drugs of any kind – even aspirin.

Answers:

Épicerie	*du fromage, des carottes*
Boucherie	*du jambon, des saucisses*
Boulangerie	*une baguette, un pain au chocolat*
Pharmacie	*de l'aspirine, du sparadrap*

**Copymaster 15
Kit phrases**

The sheet consists of separate words and phrases which can be put together like a kit to form different sentences. The activity can be approached in various ways. You may want to read through the words and phrases establishing their meaning before letting children cut them up. You may want to demonstrate first with several examples, pointing out that verb phrases (affirmative and negative) are grouped together at the top of the sheet, or you could choose to allow them to discover the possibilities for themselves. Examples of children's own sentences can then be written up on the board/ OHP and read out as the activity progresses, e.g.

Lundi je vais à la boulangerie.

Aujourd'hui on ne joue pas au foot.

On joue au tennis dans le salon.

Comical combinations can be fun to invent – providing, of course, they are grammatically correct.

CD-ROM activity 6 provides revision of the language from previous units through a series of animations.

Begin by reading through the words in the sequence in which they are listed below: left column, right column, and then the word *élève*. Before practising the pronunciation by further repetition, **encourage children to work out what sounds are being highlighted here** (é and è). Ask why they think the word *élève* is positioned where it is (because it contains examples of both types of accent, the acute and the grave). Point out how this word with its two 'eyebrows' is a good way of remembering the sound associated with each accent. Ensure that children know the meaning of all the words.

Page 39

> **Transcript:**
>
> *école, écoute, préféré, télé, géo*
>
> *je me lève, très, après-midi, poème, matière*
>
> *élève*

This last but one story is deliberately longer than previous ones, but thanks to its repetition of key phrases and its episodic pattern, should be no less accessible than the others. Most **new vocabulary can be explained by mime, gesture, facial expression or simple illustration** (e.g. *un magazine, sur les chevaux*). In addition, a number of phrases are translated in the box at the foot of the page.

At an appropriate point, ask them: *Où est le magazine? Au café? Sur le pont? A la boulangerie? Chez Madame Abdouni? Sur la place? Chez Monsieur Moulin?* Do not forget to **praise children for understanding such a sustained piece of French**.

On a second or third hearing, children could act out the different episodes.

> **Transcript:**
>
> Mathieu et les maths
>
> *C'est un mercredi. Il n'y a pas d'école. Céline téléphone chez Mathieu.*
>
> – *Allô?*
>
> – *Mathieu? Salut. C'est Céline. Tu as fait les maths?*
>
> – *Les maths? Oui. Pourquoi?*
>
> – *Je ne les comprends pas. Tu peux m'aider?*
>
> – *Oui, pas de problème.*
>
> – *Tu peux venir à la maison?*
>
> – *Oui. A quelle heure?*
>
> – *A onze heures?*
>
> – *D'accord.*
>
> – *Merci!*
>
> *A onze heures moins le quart, Mathieu sort de la maison.*
>
> – *Où vas-tu? demande sa petite soeur Amélie.*
>
> – *Chez Céline, dit Mathieu.*
>
> – *Tu peux prendre ça, pour Charlotte? dit Amélie, et elle lui donne un magazine sur les chevaux.*
>
> *Devant le café il rencontre Jean-Philippe, le frère de Marie-Laure.*
>
> – *Salut, dit Jean-Philippe. Où vas-tu?*

– Je vais chez Céline, dit Mathieu.

– Tu as deux minutes? dit Jean-Philippe. Tu peux m'aider? J'ai perdu deux euros.

Mathieu pose le magazine et cherche les deux euros dans la rue et sous les tables, avec Jean-Philippe.

– Ah, la voilà! dit Jean-Philippe. Merci!

Mathieu prend le magazine et continue sur son chemin.

Sur le pont il rencontre Benoît, qui va à la pêche.

– Salut! dit Benoît. Tu peux m'aider? J'ai oublié mes sandwichs. Je vais aller à la maison. Tu peux garder mes affaires deux minutes?

– Oui, d'accord, dit Mathieu.

Deux minutes plus tard, Benoît retourne avec un petit sac.

– Merci, dit-il. Salut.

Et Mathieu continue sur son chemin.

Devant la boulangerie Monsieur Delon l'appelle.

– Mathieu!

– Oui? dit-il.

– Mathieu, tu as deux minutes? dit Monsieur Delon. Madame Abdouni a oublié une baguette. Tu peux l'apporter chez elle?

– Oui, d'accord, dit Mathieu. Il prend la baguette et va chez Madame Abdouni, qui habite près du château. Puis il continue sur son chemin.

Sur la place il rencontre Monsieur Moulin, qui porte une longue échelle.

– Bonjour, Monsieur Moulin, dit-il.

– Ah! dit Monsieur Moulin. Tu as deux minutes? Tu peux m'aider?

– Euh…oui, dit Mathieu.

Mathieu prend l'échelle et va avec Monsieur Moulin.

– Il fait beau, dit Monsieur Moulin.

– Oui, dit Mathieu.

– Merci beaucoup, dit Monsieur Moulin, quand ils arrivent dans son jardin.

Mathieu dit au revoir et continue sur son chemin.

Quand Mathieu arrive à la maison de Céline, il est onze heures et demie.

– C'est bon, dit Céline. J'ai fini les maths.

– Ah bon, dit Mathieu.

– Salut, Mathieu, dit Charlotte, la soeur de Céline.

– Aïe! dit Mathieu. Le magazine. Où est-il?

La fête de Petit Pont

Learning outcomes	Key language	Specific grammar and language awareness
• Understanding a programme of events • Asking and answering questions about where and when things are happening	• *C'est quand? C'est où?* • *C'est à … heures sur/ au/ à la…..*	• words with opposite meanings • differentiating –u and –ou sounds

CD-ROM activities
1. Select the two things whose names in French rhyme
2. Select the answer that best fits the question
3. Allocate each word that appears to the right category
4. Find the people who fit the descriptions at the *fête*
+ Speaking activity

This is primarily a revision and consolidation unit.

Petit Pont comes to its conclusion with a *fête* such as many French towns and villages put on in the summer – not a "fete" in the British sense of the word, but several days of festive activities for all ages to which both residents and outsiders are welcome. This can be made the basis for a *mini-fête* at school, in which simple games can be played and food and drink shared. A banner similar to the one in the picture could be designed, to read *L'école de…… en fête*, and displayed in school.

La fête de Petit Pont provides a context for the revision of language learned before, and at the same time introduces some new vocabulary related to the topic.

Les fêtes de village

Anyone travelling in France in the summer will have come across the phenomenon of the *fête*, a surprisingly elaborate one for often quite small communities. The **boules** or *pétanque* contest is a typical element for the older men, this being no more than an official version (with a prize for the winner) of what they would probably be doing anyway on a summer's evening. These *fêtes* rely for their financing on people from other small towns and villages coming to them. The communal meal, often held on the main square using trestle tables and wooden benches, tends to be more for the residents themselves. One striking feature of such *fêtes* is the mix of generations: you will see old people watching the sporting events and teenagers happy to join in the communal meal or help with activities for younger children.

Begin by looking at the picture and reading the lines that go with it. Ask children to guess or look up the meaning of any new words (this could be set as a preparation task for homework). Note the term *les petits*, meaning "small children". Rather than discuss the nature of French *fêtes* in general, allow children to discover it from the information on the next page.

1 Children fill in the name labels on the picture.

Answers:

(le)château, (la) rivière, (le) pont, (la) boulangerie, (le) manège, (une) maison.

The programme for the *fête* is typical for that of a small French town. Children could be asked to see how much of it they can understand before tackling any new language. Having identified as much as they can, read through the text line by line with the class, inviting them to look up the meaning of unfamiliar words. You may want to look carefully at the times using the 24-hour clock, including how they are spoken aloud, e.g. *vingt heures trente*. Note that the abbreviation "disco", for *discothèque,* is not used in French.

Play a game where a volunteer mimes one of the *fête* activities and the others have to name it in French.

2 A series of questions focusing on the **day, the time and the location** of the events taking place. Draw attention to the key question words *quand* and *où*. Differentiate by discussing the questions with some children before they fill in the answers or even completing them together, whilst allowing others to do it on their own. Though this is partly a writing exercise, the oral element should come to the fore when you go through the answers, asking children to verbalise the day, time and place.

Answers:

C'est quand, le foot? Vendredi, à 16h00 (seize heures).

C'est quand, le concours de boules? Samedi, à 16h00 (seize heures).

C'est quand, la soirée discothèque? Vendredi à 20h30 (vingt heures trente).

C'est quand, le barbecue? Samedi à 12h30 (douze heures trente).

C'est quand, le feu d'artifice? Samedi à 22h00 (vingt-deux heures).

C'est quand, le repas? Dimanche à 21h00 (vingt et une heures).

C'est où, le barbecue? Sur la place.

C'est où, la compétition de foot? Au stade.

C'est où, le concours de pêche? Au pont.

3 CD TRACK 50

Children listen to a **time and place** and have to work out **which event** is being referred to. Each description is recorded twice. Ask children to put their hands up when they think they know the answer, and wait till most have done so before choosing someone to name the event.

1 *C'est samedi à quinze heures à l'école.*

2 *C'est dimanche à vingt et une heures sur la place.*

3 *C'est vendredi à seize heures au stade.*

4 *C'est dimanche à quatorze heures au pont.*

5 *C'est samedi à midi et demie sur la place.*

6 *C'est vendredi à vingt heures trente sur la place.*

Answers:

1 les jeux d'enfants
2 le repas en musique
3 la compétition de foot
4 le concours de pêche
5 le barbecue
6 la discothèque

4 Children should now be familiar enough with the programme of events to do this pairwork in which one asks when or where something is and the other provides the correct answer. Carry out one or two examples with a child, then ask a confident pair to demonstrate one more before getting everyone to work in pairs.

5 CD TRACK 51

Five of the *Petit Pont* **characters say what their favourite event is at the** *fête*. Children can either put their hands up to offer the answer or write the answers down to be checked together afterwards. They could then say what their favourite event would be. In order to do this, help them to identify the key phrase used in the recording: *Moi, je préfère...*

> **Transcript:**
>
> – *Qu'est-ce que tu préfères, Mathieu?*
>
> – *Moi, je préfère le feu d'artifice.*
>
> – *Et toi, Mélanie?*
>
> – *Moi, je préfère la discothèque.*
>
> – *Qu'est-ce que tu préfères, Youssef?*
>
> – *La compétition de foot.*
>
> – *Et toi, Marie-Laure?*
>
> – *Moi, j'aime bien le repas sur la place.*
>
> – *Benoît, qu'est-ce que tu préfères?*
>
> – *Le concours de pêche*

6 An invitation to **create a poster for an imaginary village fête** in children's own town. This can be done in groups, largely reusing the vocabulary from Petit Pont but changing the days, times and places. Some children may want to introduce new elements, e.g. a car boot sale (*vide grenier*), dance competition (*compétition de danse*), mountain biking race (*course de VTT*), dodgems (*autos tamponneuses*), refreshments (*buvette*), candy floss (*barbe à papa*). You could teach the phrase *Venez nombreux!* ("Everybody welcome!"). The resulting posters should make an attractive display that will also help to reinforce children's learning.

Copymaster 16
A la fête de Petit Pont

Children read the French sentences and have to complete the drawing according. They will need to draw in Domino and a cat, draw in Amélie on the horse on the roundabout, give Mathieu an ice cream and Céline a sandwich, put a baseball cap on Benoît, add a sun in the sky or colour the sky blue, and draw in some drinks on the table.

As a follow up, they could colour in the whole picture, then ask each other questions about the colours of things, e.g. *De quelle couleur est le t-shirt de Benoît? De quelle couleur est la glace de Mathieu?*

Pages 42-43

The **game** across this spread is **designed to revise words and expressions from previous units**. Each player puts a coin or counter on one of the hexagons to the left and has to say the French for the thing shown. They then move one hexagon to the right, upwards or downwards, selecting an image for which they think they can say the French. Only one player can be on a hexagon at any one time. You can only move to a hexagon for which you can provide the French. If you are stuck, you can ask for help but then have to miss a turn. The first player to reach the right hand side of the grid is the winner.

There may be a good pedagogical argument for going through all the pictures together before children begin, but the game is much more fun to play if you don't.

Of course, when they are playing unsupervised, the question of accuracy arises. You will find yourself required to adjudicate answers and to arbitrate disputes throughout the activity.

Sample answers, column by column:

Une glace (à la) fraise

(Il est) midi

Une chemise (bleue)

(Il est) cinq heures et demie

Il pleut

Un sandwich au fromage

Il fait beau

Deux euros quatre-vingts

J'aime la natation

Sud-est

Jus d'orange

Huit heures moins le quart/ Sept heures quarante-cinq

Un T-shirt (noir)

Neuf euros quarante-cinq

Il fait froid

(un) cheval

Deux heures et quart/ Deux heures quinze

Une glace au chocolat

Nord-ouest

Il fait chaud

Douze euros cinquante

Une casquette (rouge)

(Tourne) à droite

(Un paquet de) chips

Des baskets

Il fait gris/ il fait mauvais

Des/ deux lapins

Onze heures et demie

(Tourne) à gauche

Un pantalon noir

Il neige

Dix heures moins le quart/ Neuf heures quarante-cinq

Un cochon d'Inde

Sept euros quatre-vingts

Un sandwich au jambon

Contre la montre

A **pairwork activity** for children to complete as fast as possible. One partner reads out a word from each pair (from the left *or* right column) and the other must say its opposite. As well as taking turns, children can repeat the activity try to improve their timing.

CD TRACK 52 Pronunciation

As usual, invite children to identify the sounds featured in this item: *–u and –ou*.

Spend plenty of time practising them, as this particular pair of sounds are amongst the hardest for English speakers to distinguish and to pronounce well – both require the same rounded mouth shape. To make the -u sound, keep the mouth in the same position as for the *–ou* and try to say *–i/ y*. Don't forget to check that children know the meaning of the words.

Transcript:

Tu, une, sur, sud, rue, pull, jupe, super, jus

où, couleur, Moulin, boulangerie, boules, cool, joue, rouge, voudrais

Next to the lists are **two sentences**, the first full of examples of the **–u sound**, the second full of words containing the **–ou sound**. Children should practise saying these out loud. You may also like to make comparisons between the pronunciation of the following pairs of words: *tu* and *tout*, *du* and *d'où* (as in *Tu viens d'où?* "Where do you come from?").

🔘 **CD TRACK 53 Song**

Begin by playing the recording, then read through the words together, identifying any new vocabulary. Encourage children to guess the meaning of *les grandes vacances* (the summer holidays). They can then practise and learn the song.

Transcript: *A Petit Pont*

On a de la chance.

A Petit Pont

On chante et on danse.

A Petit Pont

Comme partout en France

A Petit Pont

C'est les grandes vacances!

A Petit Pont

On a de la chance.

A Petit Pont

C'est les grandes vacances.

A Petit Pont

Tout le monde y pense.

A Petit Pont

Que la fête commence!

Page 44

1 Children have to find the **odd one out**.

Answers:

a *facile*

b *règle*

c *thé*

d *beau*

e *journal*

f *natation*

2 These questions are about children's own **personal preferences**. Before asking them to write in their answers, ask one or two children each question as a way of ensuring that the questions themselves are understood. If necessary, offer a few possible answers rather than translating the question, e.g. *Quelle est ta boisson préférée? Le café? Le coca? Le jus d'orange?*

This is a good time to **play Domino dit** (like 'Simon says' but using the Domino puppet), to **revise a range of instructions** encountered in the course of Petit Pont 1 and 2. Here are some instructions to include:

Touche ton nez/ ta bouche/ ta tête/ tes oreilles/ ton pied/ ton ventre

Ferme/ ouvre les yeux

Assieds-toi

Lève-toi

Lève la main

Tourne à gauche/ à droite

Ouvre ton livre/ Ferme ton livre

Dis bonjour/ Dis au revoir

🔘 **CD TRACK 54 Poème**

A good, simple candidate for learning by heart, this poem revises expressions of weather and places in town.

Transcript:

Poème

Il pleut sur l'école.
Il pleut sur le pont.
Il pleut sur la rivière.
Il pleut sur les maisons.

Il pleut sur le stade.
Il pleut sur le château.
Mais sur la place de Petit Pont,
Regardez! Il fait beau!

Copymaster 17
Le jeu des questions

Twenty cards, each featuring a question. Having cut them up and shuffled them, children take turns to select a card and read out the question to their partner. If he/ she can give an answer, he wins that card. If not, it is put back under the pile to resurface later. The player who has the most cards at the end is the winner.

You may like to create further cards to add to the pack. Children could be asked for ideas for other possible questions.

Page 45

CD TRACK 55 Story: A la fête

This story recapitulates the names of some of the events at the *fête*. Its language is fairly straightforward and should present no problems of understanding.

This text lends itself well to a subsequent retelling with variations, which children then have to spot, e.g. *Il est jeudi après-midi. Au supermarché, Youssef rencontre Monsieur Bertrand.*

Transcript:

A la fête

Il est vendredi après-midi. Devant le café, Youssef rencontre Monsieur Moulin.

– *Bonjour, monsieur, dit Youssef. Vous allez regarder le foot?*

– *Non, dit monsieur Moulin. Je n'aime pas le foot.*

Samedi matin, Céline rencontre Monsieur Moulin devant l'école.

– *Bonjour, monsieur, dit Céline. Vous allez au barbecue?*

– *Moi? dit Monsieur Moulin. Non, je n'aime pas les barbecues.*

Samedi après-midi, Mélanie rencontre Monsieur Moulin sur la place.

– *Bonjour, monsieur, dit Mélanie. Vous allez jouer aux boules?*

– *Moi? Non, dit Monsieur Moulin. Je n'aime pas les boules.*

Dimanche matin, Benoît rencontre Monsieur Moulin sur le pont.

– *Bonjour, monsieur, dit Benoît. Vous allez regarder le concours de pêche?*

– *Non, dit monsieur Moulin. Moi, je déteste la pêche.*

Dimanche après-midi, Youssef, Céline, Mélanie et Benoît rencontrent Monsieur Moulin devant sa maison.

– *Vous allez à la fête, monsieur? dit Céline, surprise.*

– *Eh oui, dit Monsieur Moulin.*

– *Mais je croyais que vous n'aimez pas tout ça, dit Mathieu.*

– *Vous n'aimez pas le foot, dit Youssef.*

– *Ça, c'est vrai, dit Monsieur Moulin.*

– *Et vous n'aimez pas les barbecues, dit Céline.*

– *C'est vrai aussi, dit Monsieur Moulin.*

– *Et vous n'aimez pas les boules, dit Mathieu.*

– *C'est vrai, dit Monsieur Moulin.*

– *Et vous n'aimez pas la pêche, dit Benoît.*

– *Oui, c'est vrai, dit Monsieur Moulin. Mais moi, j'aime bien manger. Les repas, j'adore ça! Allez, à table!*

Alors Youssef, Céline, Mathieu, Benoît et Monsieur Moulin vont tous ensemble à la place pour manger le repas du village.

Les vacances de Noël

This spread is separated from the sequence of units to enable you to **use it at the appropriate moment of the year – or indeed, not to use it, if you so wish**.

It is designed to be read together, the illustrations helping to convey the meaning of some of the new vocabulary.

CD TRACK 56 Song

The song *Vive le vent*, **sung to the tune of "Jingle bells"**, is familiar to all French children.

*Vive le vent, vive le vent,
Vive le vent d'hiver
Qui s'en va sifflant, soufflant,
Dans les grands sapins verts.
Oh! Vive le vent, vive le vent,
Vive le vent d'hiver
Boules de neige et jour de l'an
et bonne année grand-mère!*

Translation

*Long live, long live,
Long live the winter wind
Which goes whistling, blowing
Through the big, green Christmas trees.
Long live, long live,
Long live the winter wind
Snow balls and New Year's Day
And Happy New Year Grandma!*

Les fêtes de Noël

Generally speaking, Christmas is still less commercialised in France than it is in Britain. The decorations and the shop displays appear later – and, it has to be said, often stay longer. French parents make less effort to perpetuate the myth of *le père Noël*, and it not unusual to see even quite small children choosing their Christmas presents in the supermarkets in December. It is probably true that overall Christmas is less of an event in France. New Year, on the other hand, is more significant that in Britain. While Christmas is basically a family affair, New Year is the occasion to celebrate with family and friends. Needless to say, eating plays an important part in both.

Brouillon

DH

TE

372.
654
104
409
41
ROG